MILLIONAIRE ON A WORKER'S BUDGET

FIVE FINANCIAL TRUTHS TO BUILD WEALTH

Norm Spivey
National Certified Counselor (NCC)
Colonel, US Army (Retired)

© Norman D. Spivey, 2021

No reproduction of any part may take place without written permission.

First Published 2021

ISBN 978-1-7352159-2-1 (Paperback)
ISBN 978-1-7352159-3-8 (eBook)

I dedicate this book to my family.
The real truth is, it takes a team to achieve success. We could not have come as far as we have without the love and dedication of family.

Contents

Introduction 1
Chapter 1: Planning Assumptions 9
Chapter 2: Truth #1 - Invest Early, Invest Often 17
Chapter 3: Truth#2 - Be Frugal 39
Chapter 4: Truth #3 - Collect Rent, Don't Pay It 59
Chapter 5: Truth #4 - Be Diligent 93
Chapter 6: Truth #5 - Knowledge is Money 108
Chapter 7: Truths in Action 127
Chapter 8: Final Thoughts 139
Five Financial Truths and the tips to help espouse them 147

Disclaimers

The information provided in this book is for informational purposes only and is not intended to be a source of advice or credit analysis with respect to the material presented. The information contained in this book does not constitute financial advice and should never be used without first consulting with a financial professional to determine what may be best for your individual needs.

The views, opinions and biases expressed are the authors and do not reflect those of the U.S. Army or the Department of Defense.

Introduction

The problem with most of the millionaire by (insert benchmark here) strategies is they aren't built on realistic assumptions regarding income and return on investments. Just the other day I read an article on building wealth that suggested in order to achieve a million dollar net worth, simply invest $50 a day for twenty years assuming a 10% annual return. That's investing over $18,000 per year! According to census.gov, in 2018 the median household income was $61,937.[1] That's the *median*, meaning half the households in the United States bring home less than $61,937. Investing $50 a day on most worker's income is impossible!

So how can average American workers reach a million dollar net worth in a reasonable amount of time, say 20 to 25 years? While not easy, nothing in life worth having ever is, by applying five simple truths to our daily lives, it can be done. Living the five financial truths requires dedication to a singular purpose, building generational changing wealth. This wealth will be transparent in day to day life during the near term, but will enable comfortable living in mid-life and beyond as well as provide better opportunities for our offspring.

Agreeably, a million dollar net worth isn't the end all for financial success it used to be. Inflation and consumer spending habits have made the actual value of a million dollars less than the days when "she's a millionaire" would be widely recognized as the epitome of financial success. Yet a million dollars is still a lot of money and places one very close to the top 10% of household net worth in the United States. Heck, any financial benchmark that's included in the title of a game show has got to be a respectable goal!

A million dollar net worth achieved by the early to mid-40's certainly indicates someone who has their financial future well in hand. If they continue on the positive trend, a 45 year old

---

[1] Retrieved from https://www.census.gov/library/stories/2019/09/us-median-household-income-up-in-2018-from-2017.html

millionaire will undoubtedly be comfortable in the golden years and leave a legacy for their families.

Unfortunately, many Americans today work hard their whole lives, but still remain out of reach from this laudable financial target. Additionally, in our instant gratification society, some become disheartened when unable to achieve a million dollar net worth in their 20s or 30s. Still others just don't know where to start in order to get on track towards financial goals.

I am here to share the financial truths that helped my family along the path to a million dollar net worth in about 20 years. The financial truths we'll review in this book are remarkably easy in concept, but require much effort in implementation. My strongest desire is that by hearing our story, you'll be motivated to adopt these five simple truths and get on the path to a million dollar net worth.

Important to point out, these truths include both wealth building tactics and required personal attributes. There are probably more pointed strategies for building wealth, but these truths serve as a cornerstone to achieve financial success. They apply universally and will complement more detailed wealth building strategies.

Above all, the truths contained in the following pages require commitment and lifestyle changes. Fair warning, to become a millionaire on a worker's wages takes serious dedication and sacrifice.

I am confident there are literally thousands of pages already in print with "truths" meant to unlock the secrets of building wealth. What makes this book any different? First, there are no secrets in this book. Everything we'll cover is so glaringly obvious it hurts. You may ask, "why spend my time reading a statement of the obvious"? We all need to be reminded of the simple things in life that lie in front of us but are often overlooked consciously and subconsciously.

Second, I am here as living proof the truths work. You are probably thinking, "I've heard this one before" and you'd be correct. However, see reason #1 for this book's effectiveness. I am but one of many who applied and lived these simple, obvious truths to financial success.

Lastly, and most importantly, I will use math to show examples of the financial truths in action. Don't worry, it is simple math, if it wasn't I definitely couldn't do it! Nevertheless, it is still math. Many things in life are at the basic level, a math problem. Wealth building is no exception. Math is fact and hard to dispute. To reach a million dollar net worth, the math has to work. We'll pause at the end of each chapter to review the numbers every five years along a notional subject's 25 year journey towards a million dollar net worth.

Before we begin this journey, we need to establish some ground rules for our notional subject (I call them assumptions) to base our math on. An assumption can be either validated as fact or proven as invalid. I've tried to keep the assumptions broad and flexible enough so they apply to just about everyone. I'll say it a few times throughout the book, but just because one's particular circumstances may not correspond exactly to the assumptions I've made, doesn't mean the truths are any less effective.

In writing this book, I considered creating a fictional character we could follow and observe living the truths in order to provide a little more relatability. While this would be a novel take on a self-help book, upon further consideration, I am just not creative enough to develop a fully fleshed out character that most readers would enjoy following. Furthermore, I felt it better to not assign an identity and just keep it to the study of an ambiguous, nameless subject. There is just too broad of an audience these financial truths apply to and by following a fictional character with set identities, I could inadvertently imply exclusion.

That being said, I cannot tell this story of financial truths in action without telling my own. Throughout this book, I'll share several personal vignettes of financial successes and several missteps my spouse and I made along our journey over the past 20+ years.

Our first hand examples paired with just plain old common sense will manifest itself into principles and teaching points within each of the five truths. For simplicity's sake, I will call these teaching points "tips". If someone thinks cracking the code on building wealth is as easy as just learning five easy to remember truths, then they are sorely mistaken!

A truth is often defined as "a fact or belief that is accepted as true". Truths are meant to be held to every day until it becomes a part of the values we live by, not just some of the time but all the time. The values we live by are made up of so much more than just a handful of truths!

The tips within this book are not hard and fast rules that must be adhered to in order to be a millionaire but rather serve as guides that can enable each truth and eventually lead to those values resulting in financial success. This would probably be a good spot for a Venn diagram but I'll try to restate for clarity. The tips are enablers that can help us to accept the truths. Truths are the overarching facts which shape the values that guide our lives. Don't worry it's not as hard as it sounds! Each chapter will cover a truth and the tips are clearly indicated throughout the book. Also, there is a handy reference at the end of the book!

So what are the five financial truths? Glad you asked!

Truth #1: Invest Early, Invest Often

The basic premise of get rich quick schemes is the lucky participant happens to come across a large sum of money very quickly and with minimal effort. Here in the real world, it just doesn't happen. For the majority of us, building wealth is a marathon, not a sprint. To build wealth, saving must remain a priority over a lifetime which inevitably means giving up access to hard earned income during the here and now. Psychologists might say financial planning and saving intensely for the future is a good way to develop anxiety. They may be correct, but it is also an effective way to build a fortune.

I'll cover a top level overview of the different types of investments, basic strategies and associated risks. Most importantly I hope to show clearly the time value of compounding money during our financial reviews at the end of each chapter. If you aren't an aggressive saver, become one now!

Truth #2: Be Frugal

Popular culture is full of stories about today's most powerful billionaires who lived frugal lives when they started out. One of my favorite anecdotes is of the now billionaire who used to plan travel around flights that offered meal service in order to save a few bucks. Who really knows if the stories are true, but the message is 100% valid. We must spend conservatively and always save proportionally more than we spend.

This all comes down to understanding needs versus wants and showing self-control. What it doesn't mean is being cheap. We'll explore some best practices for finding good value in our lives for services and merchandise. Living the frugal truth requires an incredible amount of patience; instant gratification is counter to being frugal!

So put that small batch, craft beer down, replace it with a domestic and strap in. Like most truths, this one can sometimes be hard to swallow.

Truth #3: Collect Rent, Don't Pay It

Ok this truth may show a little bias and some may debate whether owning real estate qualifies as a "fact or belief accepted as true". I will gladly take on the debate! Real estate makes up a significant portion of many financially successful people's net worth. More simply put, if paying rent for 20 years or more, it will be a challenge to reach a million dollar net worth by the mid-forties. Make no mistake about this truth, owning real estate and rental properties is more than just an investment, it is a bona fide side hustle.

Before telling your landlord to take a hike, please read the chapter! There are times in everyone's life when we must pay rent, but the goal should always be to own. Even better, own a handful of rental properties as a source of so-called "passive income". Our family has been very successful with real estate investing and I am very excited to share the tips that have helped us build our net worth.

Truth #4: Be Diligent

This is more than just working a double shift to fatten up a paycheck. Perhaps more than the other truths, diligence must absolutely become a life value. When something is broke, fix it…now. Don't walk past a wrong, take immediate action. When these behaviors are a part of our life values, it makes an incredible impact on many aspects of life, especially in our ability to earn. Being diligent does not necessarily mean getting work / life balance out of whack. We'll explore what it means to truly be diligent in every aspect of life.

Just working a 40 hour shift and saving aggressively won't result in millionaire status. A basic premise throughout this book is that we must continually seek opportunities and increased responsibility to be financially successful. So if the grass needs cutting or there's dirty dishes in the sink, put the book down and get to work, then please pick back up when you are done!

Truth #5: Knowledge is Money

This truth refers to two kinds of knowledge. First, and this theme recurs throughout the book, we must commit to self-study and lifelong learning in order to make informed decisions about finances. From the most basic purchases to which investment products are best, every single financial decision requires gaining knowledge and developing understanding. I'll review some of the recommended topics required to develop a basic working knowledge for navigating the road to a million dollar net worth.

The second type of knowledge is the more traditional definition of the term, formal education and training. Don't infer that a graduate degree is required in order to build wealth and become a millionaire. What it does mean is we cannot stop learning upon graduation from High School.

Without a degree or a certified skill it will be incredibly hard to increase income over the years. The best worker will almost assuredly lose out on management training to a fellow worker with a degree.

We'll take a look at the benefits of earning credentials which, at the end of the day, may only be a piece of paper, but a piece of paper that will equate to dollars on the journey to build wealth.

As you work your way through this book, keep a highlighter or pen nearby (or the digital equivalent). Mark it up, make notes and shape the truths in the coming pages to your particular circumstances. This is not your typical self-help book. Don't expect to discover a secret formula to get rich quick but rather narrative about proven truths accompanied by realistic tips that when applied, can help build wealth over the long haul.

One last point of clarification I'd like to make upfront in this introduction. I am defining "millionaire" as a person (or family) with net assets of a million dollars. Not a million dollars sitting in a checking account or a mountain of cash. For most workers, our million dollars' worth of assets will be in the form of investments, retirement accounts, college savings accounts, or real estate. All very non liquid positions. Too often we think of millionaires as sitting on a ton of cash. Not true!

Hopefully my straight forward introduction to "Millionaire on a Worker's Budget" hasn't scared you away. This is the style I'll follow for the remainder of the book! If diligence, frugality, investing, home ownership and knowledge aren't truths you feel capable of espousing, then perhaps this isn't the financial self-help book for you! But I certainly hope I've peeked your curiosity to learn more and hear my story.

Perhaps in some form or fashion you've already espoused these truths and just need a little reinforcement to help make them fully part of your values system. It is my sincerest desire to help bring some direction and clarity on how to live five simple financial truths that can lead us on the path to becoming a millionaire.

Chapter 1: Planning Assumptions

My professional background was in the military. It was my distinct honor to serve for nearly a quarter century in the U.S. Army alongside some of the greatest Americans I'll ever know. In the Army, we had a wonderful little planning tool called the Military Decision Making Process or MDMP for short. It is a staff planning process made up of seven steps that guide the staff during the development of operations orders for subordinate unit execution. As effective as MDMP is, it is extremely painful! Mostly because MDMP is usually executed on a compressed and variable timeline. If a higher order is received at 2 a.m., guess when the MDMP process starts? Yep, at about 2:30 a.m. and runs nearly continuously for the next 12-24 hours!

For this reason, many operations officers who lead MDMP will conduct an abbreviated process to focus efforts on what is considered the most important step, mission analysis. During mission analysis, the staff analyzes the higher headquarters order to determine several key pieces of information. This includes essential tasks, specified tasks, implied task, facts, constraints, limitations and assumptions. A properly performed mission analysis should give a battle staff a good basis of information they need to develop a solid operations order that could possibly save Soldier's lives during combat operations.

I share this background with you for two reasons. First, this chapter, although it doesn't contain any information about the truths, is perhaps one of the most important in the book. We can't begin our study of financial truths without considering a starting point on the journey to become millionaires. This chapter will set the context for the notional subject we'll follow during the financial reviews over 25 years at the end of each chapter.

Second, much like the MDMP, this chapter is chocked full of raw data and thus, very painful, but pay attention! Hidden within these assumptions are what could be considered implied financial tips. What do you mean?

Let's take, for example, the assumptions we will make about medical expenses. For the purpose of this book, we will assume average annual U.S. health care expenses for a family of four. This will mean generally good health and no major injuries due to accidents. The hidden tip within this assumption is make healthy and safe decisions. Watch your diet, exercise, give up tobacco, consume alcohol in moderation, don't drink and drive, wear a seat belt, wear a life vest. You get the picture.

Using this same example though, we also see where an assumption could be proven invalid. Sometimes despite our best efforts to live healthy, disease can grip a family. In this circumstance, becoming a millionaire takes a back seat to just surviving and doing what it takes for the family to heal. As stated, life happens and everyone's circumstances are different.
None of the tips implied or clearly stated are meant as dos and don'ts, but when followed, should definitely assist with espousing the financial truths.

Don't discount the truths (or this book entirely) because some of your particular circumstances may not correspond to the assumptions I've used. An illness or divorce may side track your own journey to millionaire by a few years. Don't give up! If it takes 30 years to reach the millionaire milestone at age 50 or 55, good on you! It's a commendable achievement regardless of age. Welcome to the top 10% of American household net worth. Let's get started!

Planning Assumption #1: Starting age, Relationships, Education and Credit

Our notional subject will start the journey at age 20 as a high school graduate with 15 hours of community college, single, living with roommates and employed full time as an hourly wage earner. Total of $1000 in a savings account and a brand new, compact SUV ($20000 financed at 4.5% for 60 months). We'll assume our notional subject attends part time, blended (in person / online) college courses at a reasonably priced state college from age 20-26. We'll assume the subject receives 100% financial aid that covers the cost of tuition.

At age 23, 4th year of the review, our subject will pick a partner and remain with the partner for the duration of the study. For the sake of simplicity, the partner will remain a homemaker. Two offspring will be introduced at age 27 and 30. No pets.

As far as credit goes, we'll assume good credit (around 600) starting out, building to excellent as the years progress. A quick side note, although not directly stated, it will become clear during our financial reviews how building good credit over time impacts preferred mortgage and loan rates. We will not go into too much detail on maintaining excellent credit, but the implied tip should be very obvious. Do what it takes to establish and maintain great credit!

"But I got married and had a child at 19", "I have two dogs", "my spouse works"...will the truths still apply? Re-read the beginning of the chapter! These are just the assumptions on which I based the math in the financial reviews at the end of each chapter. The financial reviews are simply a means to illustrate the financial truths in action. If you want to use the reviews as a guide or planning tool, feel free to plug in your own particular set of circumstances. You may discover positive (or negative) outcomes on the numbers and the speed with which a million dollar net worth may be achieved.

Planning Assumption #2: Employment

We will not assume the subject remains at the same employer but will assume constant employment for 25 years with periodic increases in compensation due to the subject assuming positions of increased responsibility. The subject will seek to increase education and skills throughout the time frame. Because it is public information and easy to navigate, we will use the 2020 U.S. military enlisted pay scale (starting at E3) to include basic allowance for housing with dependents (BAH) as a starting point for compensation.[2]

Years of employment	Monthly salary pre tax
19+	7492
16-18	6370
13-15	5793
10-12	5077
7-9	3866
4-6	3354
1-3	2958

For those familiar with military compensation, we will not use any of the other military entitlements such as free health insurance, basic allowance for sustenance or separation pay for our basis of compensation. Additionally, we will assume a 1.5% increase per year in salary to offset inflation. Lastly, we will assume full time employment and thus a basic offering of

---

[2] Retrieved from https://www.dfas.mil/militarymembers/payentitlements/Pay-Tables/ and https://www.defensetravel.dod.mil/Docs/perdiem/browse/Allowances/Non-Locality_BAH/2020-Non-Locality-BAH-Rates.pdf

benefits to include paid time off, available health and dental insurance coverage as well as 401k with employer matching.

Planning Assumption #3- Locality and cost of living

While the truths contained in this book certainly apply regardless of where one chooses to reside, the probability of reaching a million dollar net worth while living within the United States highest cost of living areas could be much lower. For the purposes of this study, we will assume relatively moderate costs for rent, insurance, utilities, gas, groceries, etc... If you want to achieve a million dollar net worth on a worker's budget and live in an area where average rents are $2500 and a gallon of gas is $5, it may be time to investigate other communities within our great nation!

Planning Assumption #4- Medical Expenses

I type these words as our world is gripped by a global pandemic the likes of which have not been seen for decades. That being said, we will plan for the best and use medical expenses for reasonably healthy and accident free individuals. As far as premiums go, we will use national averages for medical and dental insurance.

Planning Assumption #5- Taxes

We will dive more into suggestions on how to effectively navigate taxes at select points within the book. To keep the math easy, for the notional subject, we will assume 15% annual withholding for taxes of all flavors for the first 10 years and 20% for beyond, broken down roughly as:
- 8% (10% after 10 years) for FICA Social Security and Medicare
- 5% (8% after 10 years) *effective* federal income tax rate
- 2% *effective* state income tax rate

Note that actual withholding (especially in later earning years) may be a little higher but the assumptions use "effective" tax rates. Property, sales and any other taxes will figure in to annual expenses.

Planning Assumption #6- Return on Investment

The income sources for this study will be employment as well as returns on investments in mutual funds and real estate. For mutual funds, we will assume an average annual compounding growth of 5% after any advisor fees or expenses. For real estate, we'll use a 3% annual growth in property value. We will use dollar cost averaging and invest at constant rates to avoid market timing. Using this method, there will be bear and bull market years but 5% annually is a good conservative average return over the span of 25 years. Lastly, we will assume no need to absorb a substantial realized loss by selling mutual fund or real estate investments in low market conditions.

These six overarching assumptions make up the starting point for the financial reviews of our notional subject every five years along their twenty five year journey to a million dollars. We will dive into much greater detail on how to shape monthly expenses for our car, house, food, and entertainment as part of the truths and use the financial reviews to exemplify the truths in action.

I am certain critics are already poking holes in some of these base assumptions. That's o.k.! You can't very well have a book that contains math over time without identifying a starting point! Furthermore, and I can't reiterate enough, these assumptions are simply meant to establish a baseline for the calculations at the end of each chapter to depict the truths in action.

While your own circumstances could make the math harder, it will most likely only extend the time it takes to reach a million in net worth by a few years. In many cases, someone's particular circumstances could shorten the timeline! Many households today are dual income. Dual income families have incredibly more earning potential than single income families. You may pick investments that's performance exceeds the modest 5% average return I am using. There may be a perfect employer with more generous wages and benefits than we've accounted for.

Lastly, I'd encourage again to consider the "hidden" tips within these assumptions. There just aren't enough pages to cover every single truth and tip that can help build wealth. We are only concerning ourselves with the most important five! Live healthy and stay employed are just a couple of the "implied" tips that probably popped out. Review these assumptions for what they are and let's move on to our study of five financial truths that can help achieve a million dollar net worth by our early forties!

Chapter 2: Truth #1 - Invest Early, Invest Often

Glaring statement of the obvious, one must save money to build wealth and the best way to save is to invest. Investing makes earned dollars work harder. Although obvious, investing comes as a challenge for many of us as it implies giving up in the now to prepare for tomorrow. Investing also entails assuming some risk to those hard earned paychecks. Most of us are generally not hard wired to save for tomorrow or accept risk.

This is why invest early, invest often is a truth that must be repetitively practiced until it becomes a life value if one hopes to reach a million dollar net worth. The time value of compounding money is a proven fact and can never be underestimated. The financial reviews at the end of each chapter will show this very clearly.

I started investing at age 23, about five years too late in my opinion. My family were working class folks and in the 1980s investing was still a relatively novel concept for workers. Pension plans, savings accounts and certificates of deposits were about the depth of knowledge most folks had on financial planning. Growing up, we just never had any pointed conversations about investing. It would be a number of years before IRA, 401k, and 529 plans came into the collective consciousness of the worker. Needless to say, I entered college in 1991 without any college savings plan or financial aid.

Working a part time job to pay rent for an apartment, tuition and all the other expenses of an 18 year old were taking a toll. I cut my hours at school, while increasing my work hours, to make ends meet. This was a contributing factor that led me to the military recruiters camped out in the student union on campus. Long story short, I competed for and earned a three year Army ROTC scholarship which included a room and board stipend. This financial aid coupled with earnings from my part time job reduced the financial worries but still took some serious budgeting to make ends meet during four years in college.

There was just one small catch, I had to serve on active duty for a minimum of four years! Fortunately for me, joining the Army was one of the best decisions in my life. The military provided a wonderful 24 year career and more importantly, direction and purpose in my life which I was seriously lacking. The military isn't for everyone, but it made a huge difference in my life, more of which you'll hear about as we go along.

After graduation from college and commissioning in the Army as a Second Lieutenant, my first job was to remain at my school for about three months and recruit for the ROTC program before heading off to basic officer training. This job ranks up there as one of the best positions I ever held in the Army! Imagine, suddenly being on campus, parking in staff parking and having what (at the time) seemed like an incredible amount of money!

One day my boss, a very experienced Major, asked me to join him for lunch. He asked, "Do you know what mutual funds are?" Of course I didn't have a clue. My boss very graciously spent a lot of time with me over the next few days explaining the basics of investing. His advice, no matter how small, even $50 a month, start investing into mutual funds now. He even suggested a good mutual fund to consider and provided the phone number for more information (these were pre-PC in every home days).

Needless to say, I took his advice and am eternally grateful for it! What started out as investing $50 a month, grew to become a way of life. At our highest point, my wife and I invested nearly 30% of total income every month! We still sock the money away aggressively. There have been ups and downs over the years but a big part of our net worth is comprised of mutual fund investments of all types and flavors to include equities, bonds, commodities, international etc....

We will not dive into the best positions to hold as I am certainly not qualified to provide that kind of advice. It is on the individual investor to seek knowledge and develop a basic understanding about the multiple types of investments. I can't recommend strongly enough to dedicate self-study, at least 15 minutes a day, to grasp the basics on types of funds and returns before taking the investment plunge. What we will discuss in the upcoming tips are the types of investment accounts to open and strategies for saving as much as possible.

After a few years of investing and building a good base portfolio, I strongly recommend finding a trust worthy financial advisor. The 1% a year or so in advisor fees is money well spent to help maximize the growth of wealth, especially for those long term (retirement) accounts.

There is a relatively new option for mutual fund investing called "target funds" that takes some of the guess work out and could be a good place to start while learning the ins and outs. Gaining in popularity over the past decade or so, target funds are generally named for a target date (i.e. 2040) and fund managers will rebalance the positions within the fund based on the goals as well as distance to the target. Some of these target funds perform pretty well but most investment advisors would probably agree an actively managed portfolio with a variety of positions will usually net higher returns.

Rather than diving into an examination of literally hundreds of different investment products on the market, our look at investing will focus on the different types of accounts to establish within an investment portfolio based on the time horizon for need. I will go into some depth about how to leverage investments for near, medium, and long term goals. I'll also cover briefly the tax benefits of certain accounts and how to use this as an advantage. Most importantly, I'll stress how investing early and often is not only a truth, but must become a lifelong value in order to reach a million dollar goal.

If I had espoused this truth and followed these tips just five years earlier (at age 18) my family would have reached a million dollars in assets earlier and our net worth would be even better today. Our current portfolio is heavily weighted in real estate and we'll certainly do a deep dive into the real estate truth later in the book. But investment accounts with mutual funds were the cornerstone of our financial success and continues to make up the core of our investment portfolio. Let's dive in to our first tip to realize this important truth!

TIP #1: Close that savings account and open a taxable investment account with automatic investing for short term financial goals (3 – 5 years)

What? Everyone tells me to keep (insert number here) months living expenses in savings? Please allow me to explain. We maintain two general types of investment accounts. We have a single, shorter term (3 – 5 years), taxable investment account that serves as our "savings". We also invest in longer term (think 10-30 years) tax advantaged accounts which includes our 529 college savings plan, traditional / Roth IRAs and 401k. We'll talk more about the second type of investment account in Tip#2. If it makes you more comfortable, feel free to designate the funds in the short term investment account as "six months living expenses" but above all, move away from those regular savings accounts with the bank!

For the short term taxable account one must consider quite a bit before taking the plunge. First and foremost, how much risk are you willing to accept? The worst case scenario is to need access to funds and the account value is running low due to a dip in the market. For this reason, consider a more conservative or moderate risk mix of investments. A couple of good income producing bond funds, dividend paying stock funds and positions weighted in certain commodities are some possible options. Another possibility is a target fund set at a target about 5 to 10 years out.

We kept about a 70/30 split between low risk positions and moderate risk positions, but that is us. If uncomfortable with taking moderate risk in a short term investment account, seek less risky positions! On a positive note, even the most modest low risk funds can often return around 4% a year. A heck of a lot better than a savings account!

Remember, the goal is to not tap this account for routine or even unanticipated small expenses but rather to tap the funds every 3 to 5 years for the big, usually foreseeable expenditures in life. This may include the down payment on real estate, a car or new baby expenses. If budgeting well and living frugally, a small surplus will most likely develop in a checking account despite frequent investing.

Small is the key word here as it's never advisable to keep a lot of money in accounts that aren't growing. This small checking surplus will be what we use for car repairs, child expenses, new clothes and other unforeseen needs. Budget wisely and maintain this small cushion in a checking account to avoid tapping into the short term, taxable investment account.

On the subject of unforeseen expenses, a key point to remember about using an investment account as "savings" is that it could take about a week to access funds after a sell. This is all the more reason, to keep a small cushion in a checking account to cover immediate expenses (1-2 weeks) until able to tap the short term investment account.

The second important item to consider about the short term, taxable investment account is fees. But you said seek the help of a financial advisor? Not necessarily for this account, we'll get there! Ideally, for the short term account, find mutual funds that don't include front or back end loads as well as minimal annual operating fees. Pay attention and do the research on commissions and trade fees. There are a lot of big investment companies out there that have several quality investment products with reasonable fees.

Conveniently, these investment accounts can often be managed completely on line. Everything from linking an investment account to checking accounts, automatic investments, re-balances and trades can usually be completed easily with a click of the mouse! Account fees are another reason one should only access these funds when absolutely necessary as frequent trades will run up expenses which cuts into return on investment.

Lastly, when selecting positions for a short term investment account, one must consider tax implications. I say "consider" because that is really all you can do, be aware that income from these taxable accounts must be reported. Paying taxes is one of only two certainties in life, death being the other one. Taxes are not always a bad sign. Owing taxes on an investment account usually means you are making a profit!

Every year the investment company will send the account holder (and the IRS) a 1099 form that summarizes the interest, dividends, and capital gains received for the year. Investors could potentially pay up to 20% capital gains tax! Key to remember though, only the income is taxed and investment income is added into other sources of income. Based on filing status, tax bracket and other adjustments, deductions or credits, most people won't notice a substantial additional tax burden from a taxable investment account. That is of course, until it grows ginormous in size, in which case you probably won't care anyway!

Per my first Army bosses recommendation, at age 23 I opened a taxable investment account with a single mutual fund position. The company and the fund is still around today and remains a solid performer. My account grew steadily and compounded quickly as I regularly increased monthly contributions commensurate with pay raises. Long story short, proceeds from that single fund (my "savings") served as the seed for our first rental property purchase, other investment accounts and big expenses for several years.

TIP #2: Open and set up automatic investing for an employer's 401k (and/or a Roth / Traditional IRA); start 529 accounts for children as soon as they arrive

If your employer has a 401k and you are not participating, shame on you! 401k is "pretax dollars" and offers incredible tax advantages. Let's say annual salary is $30k a year and a worker invests $2k in a 401k account. The $2k is taken "off the top" and the government only taxes as if income is $28k! This is yet another means to lower adjusted gross income for tax purposes. This may not matter as much in the 20's but will be more important when earning increases in later years.

Like the Traditional or Roth IRA, there are contribution limits, but for a 401k the max is $19,500 in 2020! Like IRAs, you cannot take distributions from a 401k until age 59.5 without penalty. Earnings on 401k accounts are not taxed until withdrawals begin at an older age and presumably lower tax bracket.

Best of all, many employers offer 401k contribution matching as an important part of their benefits and compensation plan. Employer 401k matching has all but replaced the traditional "pension plans" that our parents and grandparents grew up with. It varies by employer but a common "match" is 50% of employee contributions up to 4% of the employee's annual pay. Using our numbers from earlier, an employer would "match" an additional $1k into the retirement account!

Important to note, these employer contributions do not count against your annual contribution limits. Any personal contributions to a 401k over the pre-tax contribution limits will count as after tax contributions.

Again I can't stress enough, take advantage of employer 401k plans and if you are with an employer who does not offer this benefit, it may be time to explore new opportunities. 401k's transfer relatively easily from employer to employer. Most employers have relationships with a financial management company to handle 401k programs. These financial management companies will typically offer some level of financial planning services for free that would cost additional if doing it on your own.

Even though I served in the military for 24 years and knew I would receive a pension upon retirement, I still contributed to the government's version of the 401k, called the Thrift Savings Plan or TSP for short. This "pre-tax" advantage provided tax savings which helped maximize our salary. A 401k just offers too many advantages to pass up!

In the unlikely event an employer does not have a 401k plan, or to become a super saver, consider opening a Roth or Traditional IRA account. This can be with the same investment company as the short term taxable investment account or a different one but it is sometimes advantageous to stick with the same company.

If opening an IRA instead of or in addition to an employer sponsored 401k, it may be advisable to seek the assistance of a financial advisor. IRA's are for the long haul, the funds can't be touched without penalty until almost age 60. That's nearly 40 years if opening the account at 20! Both the Traditional and Roth IRA have unique advantages. It's important to make good choices and continually monitor progress.

IRAs offer similar tax advantage benefits like a 401k. I am a little more partial to the Traditional IRA for the worker in their early years due to the here and now tax advantage. Roth IRAs however have some great tax advantages for the long run.

Contributions to a Traditional IRA are "after tax" dollars. After net income earned from an employer, an investor can make monthly contributions to a Traditional IRA, not to exceed $6000 per year if under 50 in 2020. $6000 is also the contribution limit under age 50 for a Roth IRA in tax year 2020. With a Traditional IRA, the investor does not pay taxes on the dividends, interest and capital gains until making withdraws, sometime after age 59.5 and presumably in a lower tax bracket.

Traditional IRAs also offer what I think is a very good income tax adjustment for the investor in the here and now. As long as annual income is less than $104K per year, for 2020, married filing jointly, the investor is eligible for a deduction up to the amount of the contribution limit. This is a pretty good deduction that could help offset the profits made from taxable investment accounts as well as income from real estate investing. If earning more than $104K per year, there is no tax adjustment but the earner can continue to contribute if desired. This is in contrast to a Roth IRA that have income limits (around $200k for married filing jointly) at which no more contributions can be made.

Lastly, I like Traditional IRAs for the younger worker because most employer's 401k plans can be easily rolled into a Traditional IRA or vice versa. In the unlikely event a new job doesn't have a 401k plan or does not accept rollovers, no problem. Just roll the 401k into your Traditional IRA and begin investing in the new employer's 401k program. While 401k can be rolled over into a Roth IRA, there are a few additional steps that would most definitely need to be completed with the help of an advisor.

These "rollovers" as they are sometimes called, do not count against annual contribution limits and are pretty routine transactions to execute through an investment company. Note, one must have "earned income" (which means a job) to contribute to a Traditional or Roth IRA account. Income from other investments or real estate does not count. Lastly, the rules are a little different for self-employed folks but they can certainly contribute to a 401k or IRA plan.

Roth IRA contributions are also after tax and grow tax free. What's more, and what makes Roth IRAs great, is qualified distributions withdrawn after age 59.5 are not taxed! Furthermore, there is no age limit when withdrawals must be made unlike a traditional IRA where mandatory, minimum withdrawals must begin at age 72. As stated there are income limitations where an earner can no longer contribute to a Roth but they are pretty high.

Financial advisors may recommend a Traditional to Roth IRA conversion at some point in their client's financial journey. While this may incur a tax burden on the amount rolled over, a conversion may be more tax advantageous in the long run. I've said it once, I'll say it 100 times, consult with a financial advisor to weigh all the options and determine which type of IRA is the right for you!

Regardless of whether participating in an employer's 401k program, managing your own IRA or any combination thereof, the bottom line is establish a retirement account now and start investing like crazy! These retirement accounts will inevitably make up the bulk of most worker's net assets in later years as well as potentially serve as an important part of any legacy left to heirs.

The last type of long term investment account I'd like to cover is a 529 college savings plan for children as soon as they arrive to the family. These plans may vary by state and the options for investment products differ, but the basic premise remains the same. Contributions to 529 plans are "after tax" dollars, meaning after receiving a paycheck from an employer, some of those proceeds can be invested into a 529 account.

Like the other investment accounts we've discussed, a financial advisor can help do the homework on 529 plans. Recently, college "target funds" were introduced, specifically designed for 529 accounts which makes for a simpler option. Account expenses as always, are an important consideration when choosing 529 investment products. The annual contribution limits for 529 plans are higher than that of a Roth or Traditional IRA.

The absolute best part of a 529 is the interest, dividends and capital gains on the account are not taxed as long as the withdrawals are used for specific educational expenses for the beneficiary. Let's say you open a 529 account upon the birth of your child and over eighteen years contribute $20000 which grew to $30000 by the time the child needed the funds for college. You won't pay any taxes on the $10k in growth as long as the money is used for designated education expenses!

Another cool feature is anyone can contribute to these accounts on behalf of the child. Grandma and Grampa can kick in $50 to a 529 instead of some useless toy at Christmas! Additionally, account owners can transfer between offspring's accounts. Let's say one child wants to go to trade school to be a welder while another gets accepted into an expensive private college. No problem, just shift some funds from one child to the other. This goes for grandkids as well!

This is an outstanding investment opportunity to pay for higher education. Unfortunately, many of us are too short sighted to start investing in a 529 immediately upon a child's birth. Some folks plan to push their children to excel academically or athletically in order to earn scholarships. Some financial advisors will even recommend to prioritize retirement investing over education saving depending on a client's particular circumstances.

I couldn't disagree more with these lines of thought and here's why. First and foremost, life happens. A child may or may not be gifted academically or athletically. They could have a tough time getting accepted into a four year college, much less earn a scholarship. Maybe they don't want to go to a four year university and would prefer to learn a trade. If so, the 529 funds could be used for approved trade school tuition.

Regardless, if the child does excel and is awarded scholarships (or any financial aid for that matter), then there are certain exceptions where 529 funds may be withdrawn without penalty, for uses other than education. Although the draws are taxed, the 529 essentially becomes similar to other retirement accounts except you don't have to wait until 60!

Other folks may be banking on federal aid or student loans. Not so fast! Let's say an investor decides to skip opening a 529 account but doubles up a taxable investment account and real estate investments. By the mid-forties (and when children reach college age), the investor could be looking at around a million dollars in assets!

It may be very likely this investor's child wouldn't qualify for financial aid due to parent's assets. This could mean taking out loans or liquidating hard earned, income producing (and taxable) assets, to pay for college. For these reasons, it just makes too much sense to open a 529 immediately upon the introduction of offspring to the family. 529 plans can be an important enabler of the "invest early, invest often" financial truth. More importantly, 529 plans provide opportunities for our children that most of us workers likely didn't have growing up. Knowledge, as we will cover later in this book, is money!

TIP #3: Establish a comfortable standard of living, then put the amount of all future pay raises into an automatic investment plan

We've got a whole chapter on living frugal coming up but this tip belongs within the "invest early, invest often" chapter. Before diving into this tip, I want to attempt to answer the burning question, how much should I invest? In the introduction, I disparaged the idea of the average American household being able to invest $50 a day, however, there is some credence to this approach.

The bottom line, to reach a million dollar net worth within a reasonable amount of time (20-25 years), you'll need to invest as much as possible while still being able to cover basic needs such as housing, transportation, utilities and nutrition. Note, I did not mention entertainment! We'll talk about frugality at length in the next chapter. If the daily amount available for investment works out to be $50 dollars a day (or more) then great. If it's something less, that's ok too. Above all, never stop investing and gradually increasing over time the amount invested!

Assuming income steadily increases over the years a worker will most likely hit an acceptable standard of living at some point. Important to note, the "acceptable standard of living" milestone could come or go at multiple touchpoints in life. For the single person, who may be sharing expenses with roommates and has very few real needs, a $30000 per year income may feel fairly comfortable. Sure, it's not living large but most likely enough to meet needs, invest some and even have a little bit left over. What to do with the extra? Invest some more, of course!

But then, love happens and life with a partner begins. For arguments sake, we'll assume the partner does not work. No more shared rent or utilities and the additional costs of family health, dental and auto insurance start stacking up with a quickness! Suddenly that $30000 per year is stretched pretty thin. It is ok to throttle back monthly automatic investments when suddenly out of the comfortable standard of living zone as long as there is a personal commitment to throttle the investments back up when income inevitably increases.

Add offspring to the equation and the "comfortable standard of living" benchmark becomes an even tougher moving target. This is why I get a kick out of the "save $50 a day for 20 years" investment plans. Life just isn't that predictable. Some years it may be $50 a day, some it may be $10. Have faith, you will get there!

Starting out is tough, I don't pretend that it isn't. Fish sticks, macaroni cheese and ramen is affordable and suitable nutrition in the 20s but unsustainable by our bodies for the long haul. The good news is, especially if espousing these financial truths, it will get better. As education and experience increase, so does earning power. Hard work will usually always be rewarded.

Part of living frugally which we will talk about at length in the next chapter is living below our means. It takes some measure of sacrifice and depriving oneself of unnecessary wants. There may be times when a worker living these truths will feel "poor" but actually have several hundred thousand saved in investment accounts! Living the truths in this book will most likely not lead to an exotic sports car or lavish lifestyle while on the journey.

That being said, there will come a time when one realizes, they are "comfortable". This is when we achieve that right balance of being able to secure an adequate amount of basic needs, save aggressively and then have a little extra left over. We must consistently self-evaluate in order to identify this important recurring milestone.

I can't stress enough, when reaching the "comfortable" milestone, at any time period or set of circumstances in life, double down and put that "little extra" into investments as much as possible. Fight the temptation to increase spending on frivolous wants or worse, living above means! It will make it much harder to remain an aggressive saver. An important key to the "investing early, investing often" truth is to kick investing into over drive whenever those "comfortable" time periods occur.

This is asking a lot, I know, but again, we're striving for a million dollars on a *worker's* budget, not a million dollars on a millionaire's budget. The $50 monthly investments are a great start, but the $500 monthly investments will kick a portfolio into overdrive. We'll see this clearly in some of our later financial reviews.

TIP #4: Invest in others (a.k.a. give back)

This is one of those tips that doesn't fit perfectly within any one of the five financial truths but best in "Invest early, invest often". You are probably already thinking, "How am I supposed to invest in others when I already invest nearly every penny for my own family?" Fair observation and I'll address that, but first would ask to broaden perspective on this tip.

There is a certain psychology at work within these financial truths. At the end of the day, the person who adheres to the truths will build "money in the bank" on paper so to speak, but will most likely feel "poor" due to the demand to live frugally.

This can weigh heavily on our minds and potentially cause us to drift off course from achieving financial goals. Worse yet, we could decide the juice isn't worth the squeeze and revolt from the truths completely. Too often workers just give up and choose to live in the moment and spend hard earned paychecks on immediate gratification.

Giving back reminds workers who are investing nearly every penny and living frugally of an important but sad fact. There are so many people much less fortunate than us. Many citizens, even right here in the U.S.A. are literally just trying to remain alive to see the next day. At the end of the day, the average American worker with steady employment has it pretty good! Giving back will keep this important point in perspective.

The good news is giving back doesn't always have to be monetary. Contributing time to community organizations, religious activities or certain causes is an effective way to give back. Donating no longer needed items is another great way to give back and help those in need.

Many workers are living a hectic day to day lifestyle making time perhaps a more costly donation than money. If this is the case, try to set aside even just $5 a week for a favorite charity. Establish a plan to build charitable contributions over time as income increases. These donations help at tax time for sure, but more importantly the personal satisfaction is tremendous.

A couple of years ago our family was finally able to start tithing. This means giving at least 10% of monthly income back to the community. The amazing thing is, we don't even miss it and the peace of mind we gain is invaluable. I hope our children will feel the same way.

Here in the real world, becoming a millionaire is a realistic, understandable and necessary financial goal. There is no shame in working hard to be financially successful. But, don't focus on this goal to the extent it lessens perspective on humanity. Give back. It really does provide clarity for just about everything we'll cover in this book.

TIP #5: Use caution with life insurance and annuity "investments"

Life insurance is often billed as an investment for the family's future. Unfortunately, it is an investment for the future that doesn't include you! Life insurance should be considered carefully and in my humble opinion, is definitely a "less is more" type of thing.

Years ago, life insurance was unfortunately one of the only means by which a worker or lower income person could pass along wealth and guarantee security for loved ones. Today, with incomes steadily increasing and all the options to invest, life insurance is much less of a necessity.

I've been fortunate in both my military career and civilian work place to have access to affordable life insurance programs offered by employers. Many employers offer very reasonable life insurance programs as part of their benefits package and it is something definitely worth looking into.

If adhering to the truths in this book, wealth will steadily build over time and when we pass from this world, those assets will be inherited by our heirs. Best case, we live to be a ripe, old age where lifelong investing has blossomed into a very respectable multi-million dollar estate. In this perfect case scenario, when living to be advanced in years, there really is not a need for much, if any, life insurance.

However, back here in the real world, life happens and tragedy does strike. If the sole earner in a family passes early, loved ones will not only be left mourning the tragic loss, but also trying to make ends meet for some time until able to pick up the pieces. For this reason, during one's earning years, it is advisable to have some life insurance coverage.

But what kind of policy and how much coverage? These are the million dollar questions (pun intended). Term life, whether it be the term of employment with an employer or a set amount of years on a policy you acquire on your own is probably the affordable and sensible solution for most people.

For instance, a $250000 policy from an employer would be sufficient to cover at least one to two years of living expenses until loved ones could adjust to their new normal and determine the way forward. Remember, they will also inherit your estate, which if investing early and often, will grow over time.

In the event an employer does not have a life insurance benefit, a 20 year (or longer) term policy for the same amount would be an option. In either of these policies, the monthly premiums would not be terribly cost prohibitive assuming the insured is in reasonably good health and not a tobacco user.

Therein lies the crux of the question about life insurance...premiums. $20 per month premiums for a $250k policy is one thing, but $200 per month for a bigger more comprehensive policy is another. If you put that $180 per month difference into a well-managed investment account, over time it would make up much of the difference of the policy value. And assuming we make it to old age, as most people do, then we get to enjoy the invested money rather than "the feeling of security" an insurance policy might provide preceding death.

There are life insurance policies with cash values, whole life plans and a myriad of other insurance products. Like many of the financial considerations we've discussed already, it comes down to a math problem and personal comfort level. This is definitely one of those areas where self-study or the advice of a professional (not an insurance salesperson) is a must. For lack of a better expression, life insurance is one of life's necessary evils, but over insuring can quickly do more harm than good for one's financial future.

Lastly a quick word on annuities as they are also often considered a type of investment that simply put, guarantees a source of income for you and / or your beneficiary in the non-earning golden years. Like life insurance, annuities come in a variety of "flavors".

Generally speaking, annuities promise to pay out a certain amount of money to you and / or your spouse, over a certain period of time based on your contribution. For instance, you may buy a $100000 annuity at age 60 that pays $400 a month for the rest of your life or until age 90 (with the assumption you won't outlive your annuity).

Annuities are generally only a good option in certain cases. Unfortunately, I fell victim to an annuity sales scam that prayed on young impressionable and eager to invest, military members. After a few years, I saw my contributions to the annuity would not nearly match the returns I would get if I put the money into mutual fund investments so I quickly dissolved the account (and lost most of my money). Lesson learned. This is the biggest reason many financial advisors will advise against annuities. Typically, retirement accounts or taxable investment accounts will generate more income than a guaranteed annuity.

That being said, there are a few instances where an annuity may be a good fit. If you are reading this book, are over the age of 60, have never invested a single dollar, but are sitting on a wad of cash tucked away under a mattress, then perhaps purchasing an annuity could be a good investment option! An annuity may also be a good option for investing the profits from the sale of a real estate investment. Worthy to note, annuities have many of the same tax benefits as retirement accounts, in that no taxes are paid on the earnings, only on the withdrawals after age 60. Investment accounts will generally offer better returns than an annuity but again, check with an advisor to see if an annuity may be a good fit for your particular set of circumstances.

TIP #6: Use windfalls to pay off bad debt or invest

Most people will encounter a number of windfall profits over a lifetime. What's a windfall? It's when we come into an unexpected, substantial sum of money. You may see it coming or it may be a surprise. It seems like some people are always coming into money, while it may only happen once or twice in a life time for the rest of us. Regardless, a windfall is generally good news! A "substantial" sum of money is of course, relative. A windfall of just $1000 at the right time could certainly be life changing.

The default response for many who receive a windfall profit is to go out and blow it on something. Don't do it! Always consider using windfalls for investment or to pay off bad debt. Key to enabling this tip is always keeping our financial life in order, so when those infrequent windfalls do occur, we are positioned to maximize the benefit.

What's bad debt you ask? High interest loans or credit cards of course. Then what is acceptable debt? Those car, home or education loans that are generally under 5% interest. Like many things we've already covered, it is all a math problem. A $5000 windfall profit should first and foremost be considered to pay off that credit card balance that is compounding interest at an outrageous 21%. But what if I've been managing my finances correctly and don't keep a balance on my credit card?

Then take a look at acceptable debt. Unless the principle on the loan is an enormous amount, it doesn't always make sense to use that $5000 windfall to pay off a 2.9% loan when you can earn 5% growth if the money is invested properly. The bottom line is make every dollar count. Always pay off bad debt but do the math before paying down principal on that low interest car, home or student loan.

Windfall profits appear in our lives in various forms. Surprisingly, government is often the benefactor. Back in the mid-2000s, the federal government had some really great first time homebuyer tax credits. We bought our first home (a duplex) in 2008 and when we filed our federal income tax that year, we received an $8,500 credit! What did we do with this windfall profit? Invest it of course!

We placed the windfall in our taxable investment account and watched it grow...for about two years. Our next duplex was only around $120000 which meant we needed $30000 for a down payment. After our $8500 windfall had grown, it made up about a third of the down payment. Isn't compounding great! Tax credits are always changing so it's good to do the research around tax season.

Unfortunately, most of us will experience a windfall due to inheritance received after the death of a loved one. My opinion is one should never consider inheritance as part of their personal financial planning. I just don't think it's appropriate. That being said, death and taxes are the only two guarantees in life. Death will happen to someone we love. When it does, try to take emotion out of the equation when considering what to do with the inheritance. Fight the urge to rationalize spending on a trip to the Caribbean or buying that new car because, "that's what my loved one would have wanted me to do". Consider paying off the bad debt first and investing any funds that remain.

I've seen this play out twice in my life. My stepfather's mother was a wonderfully sweet lady who lived the very essence of the frugal life. She was widowed relatively early but worked at a local department store until normal retirement age. Going to her house as a kid was like stepping into a time machine as everything from the clothes she wore, to her home furnishings were several decades old. Although she could cook a feast around the holidays, her daily meals were meager. Everyone knew she had sources of income such as social security and a pension, but to look at her, you'd think she was just barely getting by.

When she passed, much to our family's surprise, she had amassed a pretty substantial estate. My stepfather had fell ill due to a stroke and her legacy went a long way to helping make some needed repairs to his home and helped with the added expenses of taking care of him. Certainly this vignette speaks to the benefits of being frugal (more on that later), but more importantly, it is a great example of putting a windfall to good use.

A few years later when my stepfather passed he left me a small gift. It didn't sit idle for long until used for a down payment on another investment duplex. I know he would be very proud of all we have achieved. More importantly, every time we collect a rent check from the property, it reminds me of him.

Windfalls will happen in our life. The circumstances leading up to the windfall may not be the best, but coming into an unexpected sum of money is generally a good thing. Key to taking advantage of these touchpoints in our life is keeping our finances in order. By having a plan for windfalls, we can make a brief opportunity in our life, enduring!

This is probably a good point to wrap up our first truth about investing and dive into the first financial review. Let's see how our 20 something notional subject is fairing in the crucial first five years of adulting!

Truths in Action Financial Review #1 (Ages 20-24)

Highlights: Partner at age 23, move to new apartment and promotion at work.

	Yearly Income and Expenses Age 20-24					
	Age	20	21	22	23	24
In	Annual Pre Tax Income	35496	36028	37093	42663	43272
Invest	401K (employee contr.)	1800	1800	1800	1800	1800
	Taxable Investment	1200	1200	1200	1200	1200
Expenses (Out)	Taxes / Withholding	5324	5404	5564	6399	6491
	Health & Dental Insurance	1800	1800	1800	3000	3000
	Rent (water included)	7200	7200	7200	9600	9600
	Car (payment, ins, gas, & maintenance)	6000	6000	6000	6500	6500
	Cell Phone and Utilities	1800	1800	1800	2400	2400
	Food	3000	3000	3000	4800	4800
	Remaining for Everything Else*	7372 (614/mo)	7824 (652/mo)	8729 (727/mo)	6964 (580/mo)	7481 (623/mo)

*Everything else includes clothing, entertainment, other needs and building small surplus in checking.

Investments Summary

Compounded at 5% annually	Value at age 24
401K (+50% employer match up to 4% of annual income)	15667
Taxable Investment (Start with $1000)	8239

Net worth at age 24: $23906

Chapter 3: Truth#2 - Be Frugal

Many of us Generation X folk were brought up as children in the 70s and 80s experiencing residual impact from the economic hardships of the Great Depression. Our grandparents, especially those of us raised in rural areas of the South, were forever shaped (some may say scarred) by the abstract poverty they experienced during the Depression. They truly knew what it meant to go without, not just the pleasant things in life, but basics to include good nutrition and public services. If there was anything positive to come of this experience, our grandparents could literally stretch a penny into a nickel and they mastered the art of living frugally.

For their children (Generation X's parents), the Baby Boomer generation experienced new found economic security as the middle class grew during the boom times of the 50s and early 60s. Yet many of our parents who grew up witnessing their own parent's frugalness, also espoused frugality as a financial truth. This enabled many of these boomers to send my generation to college, provide basic needs reasonably well and build retirement accounts on a never before seen scale.

My family was definitely shaped by the economic hardship of the depression and I distinctly remember my grandparents living frugally to the point of depravation. My grandmother never ran the air conditioner even on the hottest summer days in the South. My grandparents kept a garden and cooked at home, reserving dinners out for very limited special occasions. I had one grandparent that sewed her own clothes. I recall my grandparent who dressed like it was the 1960s in the 1980s, not to make a statement, but because her clothes literally were from the 1960s. Despite enduring periods of extreme poverty during the Depression when they were young, my hardworking and frugal grandparents passed from this world not owing any debt, generally financially secure and possessing a small estate to pass to their heirs.

My parents certainly did not go to the same extremes as my grandparents, but I did see some similar frugal themes. We didn't eat out often and what we ate at home was mostly nutritious but certainly not top shelf gourmet. I watched my parents over the years save for special occasions such as an annual vacation or a new car. Major expenses were always a deliberate financial plan, never a sudden impulse. I wore my fair share of hand me downs and helped my parents do-it-yourself on the weekends around the house.

Growing up, my parents did not purchase a lot of frivolous gifts or toys throughout the year, but I certainly did not want during Christmas or Birthdays. In fact, I used to get so excited on Christmas Eve about opening gifts the next morning, I would get physically ill! I wonder if our kids today, who often are instantly gratified, feel the same way on Christmas Eve?

These values I witnessed first-hand growing up certainly made a big impact on my life and how I view finances. Being frugal is in my DNA. I learned early on how to determine between needs and wants (more on this later). I've often felt a bit out of place in this instant gratification world we live in. You'll see very quickly and through the sheer number of tips, "Be Frugal" is one of my favorite financial truths!

Living frugal is such an important truth that it must be considered when choosing a partner or it will be a challenge to make the relationship work. I was very fortunate to meet a partner who grew up with a similar upbringing and views on finances. We've mutually decided over the years to live below our means. "Keeping up with the Jones" is a real phenomenon in our society and there have certainly been some rough patches when we didn't think we could keep our relationship solid while living frugally.

Now we look at the wealth we have built together over the years and are content we will be comfortable in our golden years and not a burden on our kids. Additionally, we should be able to pass a "generational" changing legacy on to our children. But it certainly wasn't easy. Finances are a leading cause of relationship issues. Before living frugally, partners must be like minded and if not, talk about finances often. Making the commitment to live frugally must be done *together*.

Frugality has been a part of my life longer than any of the other truths but I also love this truth because it is admittedly one of the hardest to implement. Access to goods, services and entertainment is easier than ever in our modern, digitally connected world. Living frugal takes incredible discipline and yes, sacrifice. As I've looked out the window of my smaller house or been passed in my slower car I have occasionally asked myself, is this worth it?

But when one becomes hardwired to assess the utility and value of every purchase, frugality truly is the most rewarding truth and the sense of satisfaction is tremendous. In a way, reducing expenditures creates another source of income. At the very least, every hard earned dollar will work harder.

What does one do with these savings? Invest it! Living frugal means there will be times one must fight the urge to stop monthly automatic investments and spend those dollars on a want. Don't give in! Tough to master, but stay the course. To answer my rhetorical question in the paragraph above, yes I do have moments of doubt, but then I shake it off and remind myself our family net worth is much more than those with similar means who don't live frugally.

So strap in, this chapter may hit a nerve but it is a "truth" in every sense of the word. There are several tips and a lot of information to digest in the following pages. If your gut reaction after reading a tip is, "no way", pause and reflect. Make the tips work for you. As stated, these are not hard and fast rules but guides that will make the "be frugal" truth applicable and an important value.

TIP #7: Perform a "needs vs. wants" assessment before *every* purchase

If you think about it, at the base level, we really "need" very little. Good shelter, durable clothing, reliable basic services, transportation, and nutritious sustenance. Yet, we often confuse what we need in our daily lives with what we want and as the tip above implies, this conflict is present during every purchase great and small.

Let's say the candy bar section at the store initiates a craving. Ask yourself, am I so hungry that I can't wait until my next meal? If the answer is yes, then fulfill the need. If not, save $2 and ingesting way too much sugar.

That's an easy example, let's take it up a notch. Buying a car is the perfect example. Sure the leather seats, navigation and premium sound system are absolutely awesome but do you really need those items in daily life? Or would it be wiser to skip navigation and leather then invest the $2000-$5000 in savings?

Are my shoes still serviceable or do I need a new pair? Does this house fulfill our basic needs or do we need a bigger one? Should we go to see this movie or wait until it comes out on the streaming service? We could go on for days but the point is clear. The frugal mind must perform a needs assessment before spending any hard earned income.

Of course, there will be a *few* times when one absolutely should give into wants and buy the candy bar or go to the movies. We need to indulge our wants from time to time. But by pausing to determine if an item is a need or want, we will become conditioned to make *deliberate* decisions before every purchase. This is the hallmark of frugality. In today's instant gratification world it's very unnatural to pause when making the smallest of purchases, but this step is absolutely critical to the frugal lifestyle.

Ultimately, the vast majority of our purchases should be needs rather than wants. If upon reflection, it becomes clear you've been living on the wrong side of this equation, dedicate the time for some tough decisions about changing spending habits!

TIP #8: Right size your life, a.k.a. avoid champagne taste on a beer budget

I recall fondly as a twenty something Platoon Leader in the Army trying to build cohesion within my platoon by hosting the occasional get together at my apartment complex club house. I'd usually have some food items and of course, a keg of domestic beer. Even then, (mid 90's) some of my fellow Soldiers would show up with a six pack of import beer in hand. They would politely refuse my free beer for their own more expensive and agreeably tastier stash. I found this very interesting as just a few short years earlier during my own college age years, I couldn't have imagined turning down free beer!

More recently, as a landlord, I am always amazed at some tenant's homes. Many have top of the line televisions, game systems and furnishings. Also, I've noticed the HVAC is almost always set around 67 degrees in the summer and 78 in the winter. By comparison, we keep ours almost the exact opposite and have only had a few power bills over $200 per month. Counterintuitive, but I would love to see our tenants save money on their furnishings and the utility bill so they could make a down payment on their own home! Am I saying deprive yourself of the best things you can afford? Well, sort of.

While this tip goes hand in hand with living frugally and determining needs vs. wants, it goes a step further. I'll concede, you need a TV, but do you need a 72" or will a 42" work fine? No reason not to enjoy a glass of wine with dinner, but do we need top shelf vintage every day? My wife and I purchase bottles at the local grocery store for day to day table wine and keep a couple of nice bottles for guests!

Another great example where we can right size is in our vehicles. Reliable transportation is most definitely a need and one of our biggest recurring expenses. This is certainly an area where you can't skimp on quality or safety. For this reason I usually buy new or nearly new cars as long as the math works. The secret to "rightsizing" a vehicle is not just the features or make of vehicle but also the length of time owned. It will be very difficult to get ahead purchasing or leasing a new car every two to three years. Vehicles must be bought and held for as long as they are serviceable and safe in order to realize true value.

Right sizing really manifests itself in services. I am a chronic channel flipper and noted the few times we sprung for the deluxe cable package, I ended up flipping channels more than enjoying the shows. What a waste of cash every month! We cut the cable some time ago. Using digital antenna and lower cost streaming services in conjunction with our internet service, we have all the entertainment we *need*.

What's the difference between free music streaming and paid? Commercials. Develop the patience to listen to 60 seconds of commercials before the music starts and save the $5-10 per month! One of my favorite right sizing tactics is cell phones. How many folks do you see walking around with the latest phone that is costing them at least $30 per month for the next 36 months? I still use a $250 phone. It is a bit slower but at the end of the day makes phone calls and I can check my email.

Similar to performing a needs assessment before every purchase, right sizing means taking the time to determine the best value for needs. It doesn't mean defaulting to the cheapest available. Buying junk generally doesn't pay off. It does mean, when the TV craps out, take the time to research and purchase a quality TV with the features you need at a good price.

TIP #9: Learn how to do it yourself

Just this past week, I got a reminder that to be a millionaire on a worker's budget, you have to do most repairs yourself. A plumber made some relatively minor plumbing repairs in about three hours' time to two of our rental units. The bill was $700! Ten years ago, I would not have dreamed of calling a plumber. I would have completed the work myself over a weekend and saved $700. Now that I am pushing 50 and it seems like there is just less and less hours in the day, I had to weigh the costs and give them a call.

The moral of this brief story, learn how to do it yourself. I am consistently amazed by the number of folks who do not know how to perform the most basic home repairs and maintenance! When I was younger I would change the oil in my vehicle and perform just about all but the most serious of home repairs. Now I have to weigh competing demands before I can commit to a repair job. Regardless, I will still always do it myself when I can.

Plumbers, electricians, lawn care and other skilled workers charge an arm and a leg for their time. Rightfully so, they have the skills to make the dirty and tough jobs quick and simple. When performing your own repairs, it will likely be neither quick nor simple, yet it will save a lot of money. Especially, as a homeowner, the frugal minded worker must learn how to do it yourself.

If your one of those who pays a neighborhood kid $30 to mow the yard, that's about $300 per mowing season that could be invested! Calling plumbers to replace leaky toilet flush valves or painters to roll on a coat of paint in the kid's room is simply throwing money away. Over time the money saved doing it yourself is substantial. Put the savings in an investment account and watch it compound!

"But I am not mechanically inclined." That's ok, I am not either. I can't even run a bead of caulk in a perfectly straight line to save my life. But you know what, I can do it well enough. For all my bashing of today's interconnected, digital world, one outstanding advantage it gives us is the ability to learn quickly. There are literally thousands of easy to follow, professionally produced, how-to videos on the internet with step by step instructions on how to perform most home repairs.

Additionally, and I mean no disrespect, most common plumbing, electrical or other home repair tasks are not analogous to brain surgery. With a 15 minute video viewing, a few practice tries, and the right safety measures in place, most common home repairs can be performed safely and effectively by the layperson.

The biggest trade off about doing it your self is time. It will take you much longer to perform a repair than an expert. Many people are unwilling to trade their Saturday afternoon for wallowing around in the floor to fix a leaky pipe. Remember our truth here is be frugal. If you want to save money and live a frugal life, learn to do it yourself. Those saved $700 repair bills add up over the years and will help us reach a million dollar net worth.

TIP #10: Bargain hunt, haggle and use coupons / discounts

I remember as a kid watching my parents drive across town to buy gas at a station where it was a nickel cheaper. I must admit, I used to do the same thing when I started driving. I've done the math to compare savings on a tank of gas and the cost of fuel to get to the station; this is not an effective way to bargain hunt!

The most effective means of bargain hunting is being patient. Use the internet to do research. Learn when big box retailers or outlet malls have their best sales. We never really used coupons much but take the time to clip and save coupons. Don't be afraid to visit a thrift store. While selection is generally limited, they may have the perfect blender, mixer (insert unique item you'll seldom use) for much less than retail. Learn to love the clearance racks and end caps in the department stores.

Take advantage of special employee discounts that may be available to you. I was very fortunate to benefit from many businesses' military discounts over the years. Since I've returned back to civilian life, I've also used some of my current employer's retail discount opportunities. Avoid traps, such as black Friday sales. Black Friday is designed simply to lure shoppers into the store with an outrageously low bargain and then set the conditions for the shopper to make a snap purchase of a not so good deal. This is the antithesis of deliberate purchasing and the frugal lifestyle!

Retail sales are cyclical. Learn the patterns! When new fashions arrive, expect a good sale on last year's clothes. We love outlet malls for this very reason. Same holds true for appliances and TVs. Car dealers have quotas for month, quarter and annual sales. A little patience to wait for an inventory reduction sale can save hundreds when needing to make a major purchase. Making a quick purchase as soon as a need arises and paying full retail is counterproductive to the frugal life style.

Haggle on all big purchases. Haggling is a lost art and many are uncomfortable with the practice but I say get comfortable! I get a chuckle out of car dealers who advertise their "no haggle pricing". I love haggling and do not feel I am getting good value if not permitted to haggle. I will most likely take my business elsewhere. Remember it's not personal, it's just (your) business. Some sales staff may complain because of their lessened commission. I counter this by ensuring I go back to the same sales rep again and again. If I am able to make a good deal with them, they will earn my return business and most sales professionals appreciate the customer loyalty.

Furniture is incredibly overpriced and there is always margin for haggling. Not every retailer will play along but many will. Also be creative with haggling, it may require planning ahead. Let's say a shopper is in the market for a couch but the mattress is getting pretty sketchy as well. "Bundling" is an effective form of haggling that can sometimes save hundreds. There may also be financing options stores don't advertise. Don't be afraid to ask questions and be creative.

The $100, $500 or more you will save by bargain hunting or haggling adds up over time. Take these savings and go blow it on something…just kidding. Plus up one of your investment accounts with the added "income"!

TIP #11: Eat at home a majority of the time and always carry a lunch

I didn't fully realize the tremendous monthly expense for food until after a few years of marriage and especially after our kids got a little bigger. Whether eating out or buying groceries, food is a major monthly expenditure. To be frugal, one cannot eat out all the time. The small "other" food purchases such as coffees, vending machines and other not so obvious comfort foods should be avoided as well.

The *maximum* average cost for food should be around $10 per person per day and honestly it can be done for less. This allows for most meals consumed at home with one or two meals per month eaten out. Getting to this level of food budgeting takes practice and also some reasonable skills in the kitchen. The frugal person must learn to reduce waste when cooking and to love leftovers!

Let me provide a few examples. Spaghetti with meat (or vegetarian) sauce is one of the easiest at home meals to prepare. An 8oz package of pasta is around $1 and 1 lb. of lean ground beef is around $5. Sauce, an onion, maybe some chopped mushrooms would be another $3. A vegetable on the side (we'll go with chopped lettuce) for $1 and half loaf of French bread ($1) and you've got a balanced dinner for two at $11 with probably enough for leftovers in the next day's lunch. That's two meals for two people for $11! Same holds true for breakfast. Eggs, milk and bread are still reasonably affordable. A nutritious breakfast for two of French toast is around $3. Double the above numbers for a family of four.

Lastly, if you are a coffee addict (and your employer will allow it) bring an automatic coffee maker to work and brew your own. This will save hundreds over ducking around the corner to the coffee shop and forking out $3 to $5 for a mocha, latte special.

If you are thinking "I can't cook" and "I hate leftovers" then I recommend learning! Avoid gravitating towards processed foods such as frozen meals, lasagnas or "chicken" nuggets. These will do in a pinch but will run up your grocery bill more in the long run and are chocked full of unhealthy ingredients.

Our weekly grocery shopping is very simple and includes a variety of proteins, starches (potatoes, pasta, and rice) and vegetables (preferably fresh). Simple one course meals at little expense. I daresay we eat healthier than most families as we consume very little processed foods. The trick to preparing tasty simple meals comes in learning the seasonings, sauces and other tricks that add flavors your family enjoys.

Keep olive oil and butter on hand. Pick your favorite seasonings and sauces then stock up when on sale. Pretty soon, your $10 meals will taste a lot more gourmet! Over the years, we've actually found we prefer our home cooking to the overly processed and sodium packed chain restaurant offerings.

I am not saying don't ever go out to eat, we have to treat ourselves once in a while and celebrate special occasions, but do so in moderation. You may find yourself appreciating dining out more! The $7 value combo meal at the burger world will add up if eaten 3 or 4 times a week and probably take some years off a life! Make a conscious decision to eat at home and carry lunch to work. Not only will this free up more money to invest, it can also lead to a healthier lifestyle.

TIP #12: Put all monthly expenses on a rewards credit card, then pay the bill in its entirety when due

This tip is one of the most fun and rewarding in the book, but it can also be one of the most dangerous as it takes incredible discipline. To earn your business, most credit cards these days offer some type of rewards in the form of cash back or hotel / airline points. This is an opportunity for an interesting little life hack that if managed properly, results in extra "income" every year.

We went with a major hotel chain for our personal rewards card and an airline for our rental property business card. Both offer very generous points for purchases and several bonus opportunities. Let's say monthly expenses equal $2000 per month and the cardholder receives 1.5 hotel points for every purchase. That would equal 36,000 points in a year! For the hotel chain we use, that would equal four or five nights in a tourist class hotel or a couple of nights in a 5 star luxury beachfront hotel. The points program will often throw in a bonus night or two every year depending on spending and program rules.

Hotels and airlines were the best fit for us but cash back (sometimes as high as 3%) may be a better fit for many. Above all, do the research and determine where to get the most rewards, literally for your money. We have taken many a beautiful vacations with free lodging thanks to this tip.

We put every single purchase on our credit card and then pay it off every month. When I say every single purchase, I mean every single purchase. Been doing it for years. From a stick of gum, to utility bill payments, to property taxes, anything that a vendor will let us charge on a card. I will even pay the convenience fees *if reasonable*. As a result, our rewards points stack up very quickly.

Needless to say this tactic comes fraught with risk. Most financial experts would argue and I wholeheartedly agree, psychologically it is easier to spend when using plastic rather than cold hard cash. But if stopping to perform a needs vs. wants assessment before every purchase, this shouldn't be an issue. Regardless, it is something to be aware of and takes conditioning to understand that for every autopay or swipe of the card, there is a very real bill coming due soon.

Additionally, this tip requires very good budgeting discipline. One advantage to using a credit card for purchases is most cards have a 30 day grace period before the bill is due. So let's say a cardholder charges $1000 in monthly expenses for the billing cycle running from the 1st of August to the 1st of September. That bill won't be due until the 1st of October. This certainly can be an added benefit. More importantly though, one must budget correctly in order to have the $1000 ready to pay off the bill in its entirety on 1 October. If not, the card company will charge exorbitant interest on the unpaid portion and the credit card will get out of control very quickly.

A few more points of clarification. When I say rewards card, I mean one card. This is the only credit card one should own. Applying for retail cards to get the 10% off on a first purchase is just plain dumb and will damage credit. Having multiple cards especially with a balance will destroy credit scores. Do the research, pick one good card with the rewards that are right for your lifestyle and stick with it for the long haul.

If done correctly, this tip is a fun little life hack that will pay back a few thousand dollars every year either in travel benefits or cash. Also, paying off the card every month and not maintaining a balance helps improve credit score. It is already asking a lot to espouse the frugal truth. If this particular tip won't work for you, then definitely move on, but it's certainly one of my favorites!

TIP #13: Never, ever carry a balance on a credit card

I mentioned this previously but the statement bears repeating and is worthy of its own tip. Revolving credit has wrecked many a family's finances in America and more than just about any other financial matter, can get out of hand very quickly if not closely monitored. I can truthfully count on one hand how many times in my life I've carried a balance on my credit card. Not only are balances hard to pay off when the interest starts compounding, it will negatively impact credit scores which could limit opportunities to secure a home or car financing at a good rate in the future. We all will accrue enough debt in life via the big purchases such as cars, homes and student loans. Don't even start messing around with credit card debt!

What are some tips to not carrying a balance on a credit card? Well, living frugal and the tips we've already covered are a good start. You may have noticed in our first financial review, there is not a lot of margin in the budget for non-needs. To be a millionaire by the mid 40's on a workers budget, one must sacrifice wants. It is mathematically impossible to compensate for a lack of income by buying wants on credit.

There may be *very* few occasions when we have to use a credit card for an unbudgeted emergency and at the end of the billing cycle, we can't pay the whole balance off. Pay as much as possible! The interest on $200 is much better than on $800. To this point, when looking for a credit card, in addition to considering which card has the best rewards program, look for the lowest interest rates. Generally speaking, credit union or "membership" type banks will have the best credit card interest rates. Many of these institutions also offer good rewards programs.

At the risk of muddying the waters, I will mention one caveat regarding maintaining a balance on credit cards. On occasion, credit card companies will offer 0% interest on balance transfers and courtesy checks for a 12-20 month period. When used to fund something that *will provide a return on investment*, these offers are a useful little life hack.

    Let me explain, say you come across a good rental property for sale and have the financing ready to make the purchase. The only catch is it needs about $5000 in repair and you don't want to dip further into your capital. Concurrently, your credit card company just sent courtesy checks with a special 0% APR for 18 months.

    If the timing and math works, buy the property! Use a courtesy check for $5000 made out to yourself in order to make the needed repairs as quickly as possible and get a tenant into the property. Pay back the "loan" at $275 per month for 18 months using the rental income, careful to ensure the balance is paid off completely before the special rate period ends. You'll make back the $5000 via rental income fairly quickly and most likely the "sweat equity" you invested will increase the value of the property.

    The take away for both tips #12 and #13 is to keep credit card use tightly monitored. This is an imperative for a frugal life and to build wealth. If you know credit card management is a struggle for you, don't get one. Pay for everything with cash or check.

TIP #14: Control vices

Much like credit card use, we must keep tight control on vices to live the frugal life. Note I said "control", I won't say don't have vices as I've never liked a hypocrite. I had and continue to have some vices. Fortunately, I've been blessed with the good common sense and self-control to keep my vices in check.

    Whether it's smoking, alcohol, gambling or any other substances, living frugally is not compatible with these excesses. If going through a $50 carton of smokes a week, it's time to stop and put that $200 per month in an investment. I quit messing around with nicotine at age 40, about 15 years too late by my estimation.

If drinking too much, cut down to drink only on the weekend and re-read the tip on "champagne taste". Gamble once a year, if that's your thing, on a vacation and take advantage of the cheap rooms and buffets. If a recreational drug user, stop. If these vices can't be brought under control, seek help. There is no shame in getting needed help to get one's personal and financial life back on track. I have used the service of counselors. Vices in excess are not compatible with a frugal lifestyle and thusly with being a millionaire.

Not only does this help us live healthier which will ultimately reduce our health care expenses in the long run, it provides more money each month to spend on actual needs or invest. You'll see in our financial reviews at the end of each chapter the awesome power of the time value of money. That $200 saved by kicking the smoking habit will grow tremendously in 20 years when invested.

Completely unscientific assertion here, but I doubt many self-made millionaires indulge their vices to excess. For a worker to be a millionaire, the truth is they must be frugal. We can't be very frugal when blowing hundreds per month on vices. Get rid of the vices in your life or get them under tight control.

TIP #15: Beware the free lunch

Let me start this tip with an exception. Community sponsored "free" events are not only recommended but a necessity to keep monthly entertainment bills reasonable in a frugal lifestyle. Community fireworks shows, free concerts, free days at parks, company picnics and church events are all great opportunities to mingle and have some fun on the cheap. Look for these opportunities and take advantage. That being said, don't be the guy or girl spending too much time hovering over the shrimp cocktail at your company's holiday party. Being frugal doesn't mean being creepy!

Beware the "free lunch" refers to all those other "free" events that don't pass the "if it sounds too good to be true it probably is" test. Any for profit business or organization that is luring customers through their doors with freebies is trying to win business and will most likely use high pressure sales tactics once the customer wanders inside. The "how to buy real estate with no money down seminars" are a great example. Expect to be hounded to purchase books or other learning materials from the moment you walk through the door.

Just do a quick search of any on line market place to peruse the countless timeshare properties offered by people who were lured with a "free" vacation into a high pressure sales event and succumbed to the pressure. Closer to home, any time a car dealer offers "free food and games" they are just trying to get customers on their lot. Expect to be hounded by a salesperson to buy a car.

Similarly, the "extended" car or house warranty is another "free lunch" scheme that will only serve to suck away a hard earned paycheck. The basic premise on these extended warranties is they will cover repairs on a home or car after the factory or home builder warranty expires. When we read the fine print on these arrangements, the extended warranties only cover the most severe repairs such as engine or drive train in the case of a car or major structure repairs in the home.

The truth is, motors (especially on newer cars) very seldom give out. Similarly, most home repairs are minor and would therefore not be covered under the warranty. Major home repairs may already be covered under a home owner's insurance policy. The monthly fees you pay for these extended products will most likely exceed the cost of a repair.

I am embarrassed to admit, I was duped into purchasing an extended warranty for our vehicle many years ago. The $50 or so a month was really starting to get on my nerves and when I finally sat down and re-read the fine print on the contract, I realized the warranty was really only good if the motor or transmission failed! I immediately called and cancelled the extended warranty. Yet another several hundred dollars that if I had just invested, would have got us to a million net worth perhaps a little sooner!

We already talked about "Black Friday", possibly the biggest "free lunch" to avoid. Most people understand black Friday gets its name from the point in a fiscal year when most retail stores get into the "black" or profitable. Do they do this by selling crappy TVs at cost? Heck no! They get it from the ten other things we buy without a deliberate thought process once in the store. Don't fall into the trap.

Similarly, service providers (such as streaming entertainment) will offer free premium service for 30 days with an automatic payment method and the promised ability to "cancel at any time". The catch is most of us forget to cancel the subscription and get charged at least one month's fee. I know I've fell into this trap a few times before. I learned it just isn't worth the one month of free service.

Although I love to haggle, I don't have the time or patience for high pressure sales. If you don't mind high pressure sales and can say "no" regardless of the pestering, by all means take that "free three night vacation" to Florida's newest resort. Just know that a lot of folks thought they could and then suddenly find themselves signing on the dotted line to buy a timeshare they will seldom use! Mistakes like this can derail a journey towards a million dollar net worth. Beware the free lunch!

Now let's check in on the truths in action with a financial review of our notional subject at ages 25-29. Looks like their life is kicking into overdrive!

Truths in Action Financial Review #2 (Ages 25-29)

Highlights: 1st car paid off at age 25, complete bachelor's degree at age 26 and promotion at work. First child at 27. Purchase 2nd car at age 28 ($5000 sold from taxable investment, finance $20000 at 2.9% for 5 years) Significant increase in employment (junior management) at age 29. Purchase first real estate at 29 (duplex) (FHA loan, $10000 sold from taxable investment for down payment, finance $180000 at 3.85% for 30 years).

	Yearly Income and Expenses Age 25-29				
Age	25	26	27	28	29
In — Annual Pre Tax Income	43921	51495	52267	53051	70063
Gross rental income					5400
Invest — 401K (employee contr.)	3000	3600	3600	4200	10000
Taxable Investment	1800	2400	2400	2400	5000
Child #1 529 plan			300	600	600
Expenses (Out) — Taxes / Withholding	6588	7724	7840	7958	10509
Health & Dental Insurance	3100	3200	3600	4000	4000
Rent (water included)	10000	10000	10400	10400	4800
Mortgage (Principle, Interest, tax, insurance)					7200
Home repairs and upkeep					600
Car (payment, ins, gas, & maintenance)	2500	3000	3000	6000	8000
Cell Phone and Utilities	2500	2500	2800	3000	4000
Food	4800	5000	6000	7000	7500
Remaining for Everything Else*	9633 (803/mo)	14071 (1172/mo)	12327 (1027/mo)	7493 (624/mo)	13254 (1104/mo)

*Everything else includes clothing, entertainment, other needs and building small surplus in checking.

Investments Summary

Compounded at 5% annually	Value at age 29
401K (+50% employer match)	58929
Child #1 529 Plan	1639
Taxable Investment ($5K withdraw at 28 & $10K withdraw at 29)	11153
Total Investment Accounts	71721

Property #1 Purchased age 29	
Value at purchase	190000
Down payment	10000
Remaining Principle at 29	177298
Value Appreciation	195700 (+5700)
Total Real Estate Equity	18402

Net worth at age 29: $90123

Chapter 4: Truth #3 - Collect Rent, Don't Pay It

There is a reason this chapter is in the middle of the book. Get ready, I am about to "drop anchor" on this truth as my Navy friends would say! There is no better way to invest and grow ones net worth than owning real estate. Some argue this point and I'll gladly take on the debate. One thing is for sure, paying rent an entire adult life will make it more difficult to get ahead and build net worth. Why not get a return on that rent money instead of improving a landlord's net worth?

More accurately stated, be the landlord, not the tenant! The reason I love real estate is its positive increase in value over time is a sheer matter of "physics". The stock of tech companies, service providers, even commodities may ebb or flow in value, but land and real estate almost always increases. There is no more land being produced and as long as birth rates outpace death rates, inhabitants of our planet will always need a place to stay.

So why do so many people continue to pay rent and avoid taking the plunge into real estate? There are times in our lives when we just have to pay rent due to work or other circumstances. I've paid tens of thousands in rent over the years and who knows, in my senior years I may find myself paying rent again. Others may choose to live in a high cost area of the nation where it is near impossible to buy real estate except for the most wealthy of earners. I've shared my thoughts on that, personally, I would consider moving!

Also, there are two major hurdles that have to be overcome before one can dive into real estate. First, with only a few exceptions I'll review later in the chapter, investing in real estate requires capital for a down payment. Usually this is equal to 20-25% of the purchase price. This can be a lot of money for a worker to save, but by living the financial truth of "invest early, invest often" and through the magic of compounding, a worker can save the funds required to purchase real estate by their early thirties.

Similarly, to borrow money at competitive rates for a real estate purchase, one usually needs a credit score of 600 or better. If poor decisions or other circumstances earlier in life have wrecked the credit score, don't despair! Like most things, credit can be repaired, it will just take time and discipline. Unfortunately, this may require paying rent a little longer until credit scores get back up into the good range, but home ownership is still within grasp.

All that being said, my assumption is most people don't invest in real estate simply out of fear for the personal and financial commitment real estate investing requires. Coupled with this is a natural fear of the unknown and inherent risks. Most people assume investing in real estate is a risky endeavor and it certainly can be, but when pursued deliberately and methodically, the risk in real estate is easily mitigated. My hope is in the course of this chapter I can put some of those fears to rest and make owning real estate an important financial truth in your life.

The dynamic of real estate ownership has changed quite a bit in just the last 20 years. From the mid-1960s, to the 1990s, owning real estate required substantial cash on hand. This was due to mortgage rates often topping 10%! To buy a home, one had to have a sizeable down payment or the monthly mortgage payments would be out of reach for many workers. This century has seen bank loan interest rates remain at or below the 5% mark. This opened the door (pun intended) for workers to buy their own homes and more importantly invest in real estate.

Home ownership and real estate investing is a long term position. To purchase a property, most of us will have to get a mortgage for 15 to 30 years. To illustrate how lower bank loan rates have fundamentally changed real estate investing and put home ownership within many peoples reach, let's look at the principle and interest for a $200,000 mortgage (in today's dollars) at 10% and 5% loan rates over 30 years.

$200,000 amortized over 30 years	
Loan Interest Rate	Monthly Payment (principle and interest)
10%	$1755
5%	$1074

The payment, at a 10% interest rate, is nearly $700 more per month! Add to the monthly principle and interest payment, the property taxes, (typically around 2% of the home's value per year), maintenance and upkeep costs as well as homeowner's insurance and it is easy to see why real estate owner ship was out of reach for most workers just a few years ago.

Thankfully, interest rates in the 5% or lower range have been here for a while and there is no indication we will go back to 10% or greater mortgage rates. Many people have been able to take advantage of this opportunity over the past 20 years. With the exception of a few recession periods, home ownership is steadily increasing thus far in the 21st century. This has fundamentally changed for the better our culture.

With more Americans having access to financing, comes the construction of more homes to meet the demand. While this is still overall a good news story, the result is cookie cutter developments and "spec" homes. Around these developments, come commercial real estate, usually in the form of strip malls that provide local residents' life's necessities. What in many cases was beautiful raw land just a couple of decades ago, is now urban sprawl. Furthermore, as raw land to build these communities is depleted, home prices go up, many times offsetting any opportunities created by low interest rates.

Which brings me to a point. Too many people today, define success as being able to buy a 2000 square foot single family home in one of these stamped out communities in the suburbs while still in their 20s. For me, this is a very short sighted approach to real estate investing and home ownership.

Don't get me wrong, every citizen has the right to pursue happiness. If purchasing a small single family home as quickly as feasible is what will bring happiness, then go for it. In most cases however, people who spend their hard earned money on these "starter" homes in their 20s or early 30s will quickly outgrow the residence and begin longing for something more. This is a phenomenon commonly known as "keeping up with the jones". Additionally, families have an uncanny way of growing in size!

The first time home owner could find themselves tying up their capital in a starter home and squandering an opportunity to fully realize the investment potential of real estate. Too many people these days are looking for instant gratification and the thought of waiting for a nice home until their 40s is unfathomable. I was 42 when we bought our first single family home!

I believe there is a better approach to owning real estate. Pay rent in the 20s, work hard, live frugal, save aggressively and purchase a first home in the early to mid-30s that will become the cornerstone of a profitable real estate investment portfolio. Simply put, make your first real estate purchase an investment property, preferably multi-family. Then, when approaching mid-life, buy that dream home you've always wanted and now have the means to afford!

We have already talked about many of the sacrifices required to live these five financial truths and become a millionaire on a worker's budget. The real estate truth is no different and in fact, may require some of the biggest sacrifices of all. Even more so than living frugally, "collect rent, don't pay it" was the toughest truth for our family to implement. Before we get into some practical application examples and tips to help live the real estate financial truth, I need to share our family's real estate investing journey.

Bouncing around from post to post every two to three years in the military, sometimes overseas, makes it a challenge to buy a home or invest in real estate. In my 24 years of service I spent over eight years overseas! Some service members are able to purchase homes and invest in real estate but most are not.

Fortunately, my wife and I were able to start our real estate investing while on active duty, but it certainly wasn't easy. Both of our families had dabbled in real estate investing when we were growing up. While neither of us came from wealthy circumstances, what little net worth our families had amassed, came almost entirely from home ownership. We both decided home ownership and rental property investing were an important part of our financial goals when we tied the knot in 2001.

The Army had other plans. We married while stationed in Germany, so not many opportunities to invest. When we came back to the states, my next four year assignment required that we live in on-post housing. After departing that station, my next assignment (albeit only a year) also required living on post!

In 2008 we had been married seven years, had two small children and had paid rent our whole adult lives up to that point. I was 35 years old and my wife was 38. We were ready to own a home! But again, the Army gets a vote. Our next assignment was to Ft. Hood, TX. On a positive note, central Texas real estate was extremely affordable at the time due to an abundance of land and low construction cost. On a negative note, we learned that I would be deploying within two months after arriving to Ft. Hood!

It was at this time we made the conscious decision to make our first real estate purchase a duplex. I would be gone for the first year of our assignment to Ft. Hood so the wife and toddlers didn't need much space. The kids weren't even in school yet! City zoning in Killeen, TX resulted in an abundance of nice multi-family properties mixed in with single family neighborhoods rather than massive apartment complexes.

Additionally, our seven years of frugal living and investing early and often had racked up a good bit of capital in our taxable investment account. We could afford a 25% down payment for an investment property. We would live in one side of the duplex and rent the other. The rental income we gained would cover our mortgage, insurance and taxes while the portion of our pay the Army designated for housing allowance would go into our pockets, or more accurately, back into our taxable investment account.

Sounds like a no brainer right? This is where the human factor and the sacrifice comes in. We were nearly 40 years old and had never owned a home. We were blessed to have risen in rank to Major which certainly didn't make us wealthy but we were comfortable. Most people in our circumstance bought lovely, new construction, single family brick homes in the area.

We instead chose to live in one side of our duplex, a 1200 square foot apartment, and put our families' long term financial well-being as the priority. My wife couldn't invite people over and when she did some of the more catty spouses would remark, "how can you live like this"? The house was tiny and we barely fit. There were a lot of tears, but we made it!

One of the upsides to deployments is it offers an opportunity to save a ton of money. This coupled with the income we were making in our first duplex enabled us to save enough to buy another duplex shortly after I returned from deployment. We were very fortunate to find a distressed property (more on this topic later) at a great price. Even though I had to spend a week fixing it up before we could offer it for rent, this duplex has since become one of our best performers.

I got to stay home about seven months before I had to deploy again. While me being out of the picture gave the wife and kids more room in our 1200 square foot duplex home, raising two small children alone and managing two rental properties was taking its toll on her. This is when we established a great relationship with a local property management company that we still maintain today.

You'll see in the financial review at the end of this chapter how real estate income starts stacking up quickly and our experience proved this out. With the additional income from our two duplexes and the money we were saving by me being deployed, the wife went out, on her own I might add, and found yet another duplex to purchase in the area. I arrived back from the deployment just in time to make it to closing!

We had acquired three duplexes in central Texas over a four year period at good purchase prices. The rental market was red hot at the time (as it remains today) and the properties were turning a profit. Perhaps it was finally time to move out of the duplex and find a nice single family home for our growing family.

But again, the Army gets a vote. We received orders for another overseas assignment. Back to renting! While we were overseas for two years, our properties in Texas continued to flourish and we invested the rental income in our taxable investment accounts which compounded the profits nicely. If you are doing the math here, all of this occurred during the recession period in the 2008-2012 timeframe. Our family finances weathered the recession with no significant issues. Towards the end of our overseas assignment, we received our next orders, Washington, D.C.

While we loved living in the D.C. area, we also experienced some sticker shock at the prices of homes. Not knowing what the military had in store for us, we decided not to buy and paid rent yet again. This proved to be a very fortuitous decision as the Army decided to move us again after only one year in D.C. In a very fortunate turn, we received orders for Redstone Arsenal, in Huntsville, AL.

Huntsville's claim to fame is the Marshall Space Flight Center where much of the development on the Saturn V rockets that took Americans to the moon was completed. Huntsville truly is an oasis within the Tennessee River Valley. There are numerous large and small defense industry businesses located here which draws engineers, scientists and professionals from all over the country. Some people say there is a higher density of PhD's in Huntsville, AL than anywhere else in the nation!

On top of all that, cost of living was great and there were new home developments seemingly on every corner. In 2015 at the age of 42 we bought our first single family home! Still not knowing what the future held as far as our military service, we bought our first home using the same thought process as our investment properties, treating it purely as a business deal. Boy was that a mistake! Let's just say when it does come time to buy your first real home, make it count!

Looking around the Huntsville area, we noticed that investment properties to include small condos and multifamily duplexes were very reasonably priced. Through some good timing and creative financing we'll cover in the upcoming tips, we were able to purchase three small single family condo units and three duplexes over the next four years.

Unlike our investment properties in central Texas, we actively managed our north Alabama properties which ended up providing my wife with a nice part time job, a nice change of pace for her. She previously worked as a homemaker for most of our time in the military.

When it came time to pack up and leave again on the next military adventure, our family had reached a critical cross roads. We landed, quite by accident, in a portion of the country that had a lot to offer. Our kids were at the age where friends are everything and they liked the schools. We had already invested heavily in the area. Post military jobs were plentiful. Although it was a tough decision, it just made sense for our family to get off the military train after 24 years of service.

When we retired in 2019 our real estate portfolio included our personal residence, three duplexes in Texas, three duplexes and three condos in North Alabama. We also started to make plans for building another duplex. New construction has been an adventure all to itself, perhaps a topic for a whole other book!

In just over ten years we had amassed over a million dollars in real estate equity enjoying over a 300% return on our initial investment. Important to note, "initial investment" is a bit misleading. Really only maybe our first two or three properties were bought with money that I actually received a paycheck for and then used to purchase real estate.

For the most part, we funded the acquisition of our real estate investments using income from our existing portfolio, sort of a snowball effect if you will. We reinvested all of our income from real estate for 10 years. Only recently have we started taking small draws each month. As we push 50 years old, it seemed like time to enjoy some of the fruits of our labor!

We made several mistakes along the way to be sure, but definitely got it right more than we screwed up. Not sure how much of our successful real estate portfolio was luck and how much was skill but regardless, we are very blessed and thankful. I am very eager to share with you in the following pages some of the tips that made owning real estate such a successful financial truth for our family.

But first, in case this personal account on the benefits of real estate was not enough, I want to review why "collect rent, don't pay it" is a financial truth to become a millionaire on a worker's budget. To fully realize the benefit of real estate investing, one must understand the three ways real estate generates income.

1. Rental income. How much income a property will produce depends on numerous variables we will go over during the tips portion of this chapter. Regardless, a good investment property should produce some level of income, meaning that the monthly rents collected should equal more than the outgo for mortgages, insurance, taxes, maintenance and any other expenses. The IRS will refer to real estate income as passive. I assure you, nothing is "passive" about real estate investing! From the moment of first viewing the listing when shopping for an investment property to picking up a monthly rent check, every aspect of real estate investing involves a decision or action. Think of it as a part time job and it won't sting as bad when receiving a call from an angry tenant about a broken HVAC at 9pm on a Sunday night! Ideally, any net income earned from real estate is rolled back into a taxable investment account or tax deferred retirement account which makes the profits compound even more. Rental income is taxable which brings me to the second way real estate investing provides a unique benefit.

2. *Tax benefits.* There are tax advantages to owning real

estate which we will cover in detail during the tips. In a way, the tax benefits of rental income make it similar to the tax benefits offered by investing in a 401k, sort of a "pre-tax" benefit. Although a landlord may collect $10,000 in gross rental income, after deducting expenses and depreciation for a particular property, the actual taxable income is MUCH lower. These tax savings add up over time and increase the "earning" power of an investment portfolio. We will look at this in depth in the coming pages.

3. **Building Equity.** This is my personal favorite and can be maximized in several ways. Simply put, equity is the difference between what the property is worth and how much owed to the bank. Essentially, a portion of monthly collected rent checks pass through the investor to the bank paying down principal and thusly building equity. We will take a look at creative means to finance investment properties that make this process more efficient. Additionally, property values will almost always increase. Multi-family property value won't increase as quickly as single family homes but will increase nonetheless. There are also "sweat equity" improvements a property owner can complete to improve the condition of a property making it more valuable. Obviously, the more sweat equity an owner can do on their own, the more return on the improvement. An old saying goes, "you make your money from real estate when you buy it". We'll explore how to build equity in detail.

There is a reason "invest early, invest often" was the first truth we covered. A large portion of our net worth is invested in mutual funds. In case you missed it, we could not have invested in real estate if our "savings" in taxable investment accounts had not grown to a level where we were able to make a down payment on that first property. Additionally, I don't think anyone would ever recommend putting all eggs in one basket. Owning a mix of investments to include mutual funds and real estate is the best portfolio to build wealth and become a millionaire on a worker's budget. Collecting rent and not paying it is a challenging but rewarding financial truth. Enough of the preface, let's dive into some tips that will help "collect rent, don't pay it" become a truth in your life!

> **TIP #16:** The first rule of real estate is location, location, location; the second rule of real estate is location, location, location

I know its clichéd but it is absolutely true. If money is made from real estate when the asset is acquired, then no single factor is more important than where the property is located. Fortunately, the same factors that drive up home prices are what impacts rental markets.

When choosing an investment property, this is certainly a case where cheaper is not always better. Cheap properties will pull cheap rent and more than likely will lead to more headaches than the amateur investor wants to deal with. Ideally, finding a multi-family property that is not located in a high density multi-family area, but rather mixed in among single family homes is perfect.

Many cities tend to keep multi-family dwellings zoned separately from single family homes. We were fortunate that our first duplex was a new construction set on a street with other duplexes within a community of predominantly neat little brick single family homes.

Finding a city such as Killeen, TX that zones in this manner is unique but there are some. Regardless, if a multi-family property is sitting in an undesirable part of town, it will be very slow to increase in value or rents. Look for a multi-family located adjacent to or just at the edge of desirable single family neighborhoods.

Like single family housing, one of the biggest factors that determines rents and purchase price is schools. Homes zoned for well rated public schools will increase in value and pull more rent. School zoning is the first thing we look at when purchasing a property.

We are always wary of fixer uppers, but an ugly duckling at the right price in an amazing location may be worth the gamble. Our second duplex was a bank owned property and had been vacant for a few years. The worst thing that can happen to a home is to set empty! It sat in a great neighborhood with good schools so we made a low ball offer and surprisingly the bank accepted. Took a week off from work and 10 hour days fixing it up but we've kept that property rented ever since and it has almost doubled in value!

We completed a similar deal in Huntsville, AL on a small condo unit that was distressed. If going the fixer upper route, recall what I mentioned in the "frugal" chapter. Learn to do it yourself or margins will quickly shrink. I don't always recommend fixer uppers, but if they are located in the right area it's worth a consideration. One note, when assessing a property and determining it needs $5000 worth of work…add another $5000 for items that are lurking just under the surface!

There are several other factors to location for investment properties that are mostly common sense. Multi-families located in rural areas with long commutes to employment, restaurants, grocery and retail won't be easy to rent. That doesn't mean all rural areas are bad investments as it really depends on the type of property.

A one bedroom / one bath duplex apartment in a rural setting will have a very small market of potential renters. Younger, single people usually wouldn't be interested in this type of home as it is farther away from work and entertainment. Perhaps a single, retired person would be interested in renting a one bedroom in a rural setting which is certainly ok. But how many single, retired people are looking for apartments at any given time? The same one bed / one bath apartment in the middle of a city may demand a high rent and have a waiting list of prospective tenants!

On the other hand, a three bedroom, two bath in a rural setting that is a reasonable commute to the city but also zoned for good county schools may rent quickly. Many families want to take advantage of the county school system and get their kids out of an urban area. Some single folks may look to take on some roommates in order to save some money and would be willing to move a little further out of town. The point is, consider the market for prospective tenants based on the location and type of home.

This is good old fashioned market analysis and must be completed before the purchase. Fortunately, analyzing rental markets is mostly common sense and there are tools available to help. There are a lot of good apartment finder web sites that can be used to find comparable rents in the area to determine rental potential. Additionally, there are many web sites that will provide demographic data to include income, family size and age for a particular area. With just a few quick internet searches, it is easy to determine if a particular area has a high density of families, retirees or single workers.

The bottom line of all this is location, location, location determines rent, rent, rent which once you factor in the various expenses reveals how valuable an investment property will be. There is a formula for figuring this called capitalization rate which is simply the net income (rent after subtracting all expenses) divided by the value of the asset and expressed as a percentage. For instance, if annual net rental income for a property is $10000 and the property is valued at $100000 then the cap rate is 10%. Generally you want to be in the 8-10% cap rate range to make a good real estate investment.

There are numerous ways to calculate cap rate and I recommend figuring it conservatively by using maximum projected expenses and minimum expected rents. When considering a property, determining cap rate goes hand in hand with location, location, location and is an important first step before making an offer. Once the real estate investor gets this figured out, everything else about real estate investing should fall right into place!

TIP #17: Understand financing options and don't be afraid to get creative

Critical to making money on real estate during the purchase is financing. I always get a chuckle out of these "buy real estate with no money down" seminars that roll through town from time to time. What a half-truth! Most banks will only go 75% loan to value on an investment property loan which means when securing a conventional mortgage from the bank, 25% down payment will be required. Conventional mortgages for investment properties also will have slightly higher interest rates than a loan for an owner occupied property. Makes sense, the bank is just covering its interest. It is a lot easier for someone to walk away from an investment property than their own home!

Additionally, conventional mortgages will only work for one to four unit investment properties. Anything over a four unit structure (quadraplex) and a business loan will be required. Generally speaking, business loan terms are a little tougher for the individual investor and can include a balloon payment after 5-7 years.

So what's the good news? If you have good credit and are disciplined, there are creative ways to finance properties at reasonable interest rates that can increase the profitability of an investment. First, low or no money down loans are great for owner occupied properties. Qualifying individuals can use VA, FHA and other government secured loans for investment properties if the buyer resides in the property. These loans require little to no money down and usually banks will offer attractive interest rates for government backed loans.

If the owner moves out of the home, not to worry, the mortgage remains in place at the great interest rate! Important to remember, the less down payment, the more the monthly mortgage will be which cuts into return on investment for the property. For a first time investor though, a government backed loan is definitely the best way to get into real estate investing without using up a big chunk of capital.

A more creative way to finance a real estate purchase may be to borrow money using investment accounts or retirement accounts as collateral. Can't stress enough that this takes incredible discipline since failing to pay back the loan will result in forfeiting a large part of retirement or investment savings, sometimes with additional penalties. That being said, interest rates for these types of loans are usually decent and in some cases, such as with the government employee's Thrift Savings Plan (TSP), the interest rate is outstanding. Be sure to read the fine print as there may be restrictions on what these loans can be used for.

Going this route will usually require some out of pocket capital to make up the complete purchase price, but on a positive note, the property will be owned outright as there won't be a mortgage against the property. Additionally, these types of loans usually won't show up on a credit report.

We purchased a small single family condo that was distressed for $36k and used a $40k loan from our TSP account to pay the purchase price and the $6k in needed repairs. Although we didn't make any profit on this property initially, the rental income was enough to pay back the loan in just a few years. Also in that time, the value of the property nearly doubled! The funds used from our TSP loan had yielded a much higher rate of return than if we had left it sitting in the retirement account! We made a similar profitable property purchase a couple of years later by using a loan with our taxable investment account as collateral. Of course, when offering up an investment account as collateral, the funds can't be accessed so be sure to have a plan!

Still another creative way to finance investment properties is the use of credit card or personal loans. This is absolutely a risky venture and takes incredible discipline. If you have good credit and receive those special 0% courtesy check offers for periods of greater than 18 months, then this might be an option.

It is imperative to pay off credit card loans during the 0% introductory period as the interest rates for credit card loans are enormous. Additionally, these types of loans will most definitely appear on a credit report as revolving debt which could negatively impact the score. Also, read the fine print as there are sometimes limitations on what credit card or personal loans can be spent on. I just can't stress enough, these types of loans present incredible risk, be sure to consider every angle before pursuing this option.

We purchased a small single family condo using a $25k, 0% credit card loan for 18 months along with $25k cash from our taxable investment account. Although the rental income didn't completely cover the $1400 each month required to pay off the credit card loan, we used income from our other properties to make up the difference. We paid off the credit card loan using rental income during the 18 month introductory period. The property is a proven performer and like our other homes is steadily increasing in value!

The bottom line is getting financing together prior to purchase is an absolutely critical step to real estate investing. Securing a conventional loan with crappy terms or worse yet getting sideways on a creative finance arrangement can not only make real estate investment not profitable, but potentially financially ruinous. Do the homework and maintain a good understanding of all the financing options.

TIP #18: Maintenance, repairs and the general cost of ownership must be kept under control to remain profitable in real estate investing

Much like determining a good location, before purchasing an investment property, the real estate investor must make an accurate assessment on how much will be required to maintain the property. We talked briefly about how this figures into determining a cap rate for potential investment properties. Before making an offer, be able to determine the condition of big items at a glance- roof, HVAC, water heater, windows. Also the little stuff that is relatively easy repairs: paint, blinds, light fixtures, appliances. Know the general cost of repairs, both major and minor. If at least $5k in repairs jumps out immediately, realize there are probably another $5k lurking just under the surface. This may not be the right property!

Once an offer is made and the buyer is under contract, there are thankfully many licensed home inspectors that for a well spent $300-$500, can provide a detailed inspection on a property before closing. Find a good home inspector and don't skip this critical step! If the inspector comes back with a bad report, don't be afraid to walk away from the deal.

We had to walk away from a deal for a single family home that we intended to live in. The home had beautiful upgrades as we learned the owner was a skilled craftsman. The only problem, there were no permits for the updates and several were not within local building code. If we had not had a thorough home inspection, we may not have been able to secure financing or worse yet entered into a potential money pit trying to bring the property up to code!

In addition to repairs and maintenance, some properties may require monthly Homeowners Association (HOA) dues. These are usually townhouse or condo style properties but may also apply to single family homes in certain subdivisions. Gain a full understanding of what the HOA dues cover and make an assessment if the dues seem reasonable. HOA dues will often cover, water, sewer and trash pickup as well as common area maintenance and lawn care. We were fortunate to find some condos with fairly priced dues and after deducting expenses from gross rent, we were still able to turn a profit.

HOAs are all managed a little differently and the dues may not always be reasonable. If the math doesn't add up, don't be afraid to pass on the property. Additionally, be aware that condos will levy special assessments from time to time for major repairs such as replacing roofs or repaving sidewalks. While it's hard to predict when the assessments may occur, it is a safe assumption that if the property's roof looks to be in rough shape and the sidewalks are badly cracked, there are assessments coming in the near future. HOA dues and special assessments are non-negotiables, if purchasing a property that is part of an HOA the owner must pay the dues. Failure to do so could result in a lien placed against the property by the HOA management.

To be a successful real estate investor, do it yourself skills are a must. Replacing a flush valve (the guts inside a toilet tank) is a relatively simple job that takes about $10 in parts and 15 minutes of time. But a plumber will charge around $100. Similarly, once the prep work is complete, slapping on a coat of paint is pretty easy. Installing blinds, light fixtures and basic plumbing are simple tasks the layperson can perform after watching a few videos on the internet. As for yard work and move out cleaning? Don't even think about hiring it out!

The bottom line is if an investor outsources every single maintenance, cleaning and repair job, it will be very hard to stay profitable on real estate investments. There are enough major repairs such as water heaters and HVAC systems where an expert will have to be called in. This is why I get a kick out of the term "passive" income. Actively managing and maintaining rental properties is anything but passive. It is a bona fide part time job!

There may be times when an investor may relocate and have to turn over management and maintenance of a property to a property management company. Expect around a 10% fee on gross rental income for management service. Fortunately, there are usually some good property managers in just about every city. We've used a property manager successfully for over a decade for our properties in Texas.

The key is stay in constant communication with the property manager and watch maintenance dollars very carefully. Evaluate constantly. Question everything and understand enough about repairs to know if someone is trying to pull wool over your eyes. Even if everyone is on the up and up, due to the additional maintenance and management costs it may become necessary to divest of a distant property and reinvest locally. We've been fortunate to work with a great property manager over the years and are able to keep our distant real estate holdings profitable.

Lastly, a word on deferred maintenance. Never walk past a serious maintenance issue (more on this later in our chapter on diligence) and above all, ensure you are providing tenants a safe, clean, serviceable home. They are paying a lot of their hard earned money to live in a good home. Do not betray their trust by ignoring maintenance problems.

There may be a very few occasions when it just makes more sense to defer a maintenance item until a tenant moves out based on the scope of the repair. I've found this is the exception more than the rule. It's just best practice to address maintenance issues immediately. Not only is it the right thing to do, your tenants will appreciate you for it and take it into consideration when it comes lease renewal time!

TIP #19: Understand and leverage rental property income tax implications

Whether deeded in the name of a LLC or the owner's name, rental income is accounted for on our personal income tax return. While it's pretty straight forward, before investing in rental property, I highly recommend consulting a tax professional or using tax software designed for rental property owners. We use tax software and have not had any issues.

At the very basic level, the tax paid on rental property income is based on the difference between the gross collected rent and the expense to operate and maintain the property as a rental. This is where it gets exciting! The definition for these expenses is fairly broad. This is one distinct advantage real estate investments hold over traditional market based investments. Most people can't write off investment account expenses anymore. Additionally, and this is the best part, the IRS has some unique rules for determining expenses. Let's dive in!

Repairs, maintenance and cleaning are pretty straight forward. If paying someone to fix a leaky faucet or clean a property, the cost of the bill is deductible from the gross income. Similarly, if the owner makes the repairs, the cost of the materials for the repair as well as in some cases even the tools are deductible! If repairs are major, generally defined as costing more than $2500, such as replacing an HVAC, roof or new windows, then the repair becomes real property that can be depreciated over time (more on depreciation coming up).

Cleaning supplies, a box of nails, a gallon of paint or a bag of grass seeds are all examples of materials which are commonly deducted as expenses to maintain or repair a rental property. You may ask, well how does the IRS know if I use all of the cleaning product on the rental property? Only the cost of the materials that are used for the rental property are supposed to be deducted….and that is all I am going to say on this point!

Similarly, if one of the appliances craps out and it's time for a new one, the cost to replace that refrigerator, oven or dishwasher can be written off as a repair. This presents an excellent opportunity to upgrade to nicer appliances that will potentially help increase rents or resale values. The investor gets the benefit of putting some "sweat equity" into the property as well as a tax write off! A quick note on this point, remember it is only repairs. While an owner can certainly add a deck or patio to a rental property, those are improvements and not deductible!

The other common deductions are what I call the price of doing business items. This includes insurance premiums, HOA dues, property taxes and my personal favorite, mortgage or business loan interest! There are some other price of doing business expenses out there that are also deductible but they must be directly related to owning and maintaining the rental property. This could include certain property management tools, PO boxes, business taxes and other items or services needed to operate the rental. I've said it once, I'll say it again, check with a tax professional if any questions!

One expense I particularly love is mileage deductions. As of 2020 the IRS mileage deduction is .58 cents per mile. If a property is located on the route to work and the owner stops by to show, repair or otherwise manage the rental on their commute, then that portion of the route is deductible! Similarly, if making a trip to the local big box to pick up material for repairs or really any other rental related errand, those trips are deductible! What if I buy something else for personal use while I'm at the big box? Read between the lines!

Mileage expense adds up very quickly and I daresay it doesn't cost exactly .58 cents a mile to operate a vehicle.

Planning business mileage wisely is an excellent way to realize the tax benefits of rental property ownership. That being said, the IRS does require well documented mileage reports for these trips. Thankfully there are some awesome smartphone apps that help manage the task. Just keep the app running in the back ground and it will capture all daily trips, then at the end of the day, review each trip and designate which ones were rental property related and which ones were personal. We've averaged over $2000 in deductions each year on business mileage!

Lastly, my favorite deduction from rental income is depreciation! Depreciation is simply reducing the value of a certain property over its useful life. Real estate can be depreciated over its useful life, a maximum of 27.5 years as currently determined by the IRS and can be depreciated all the way down to zero. The most common means for determining depreciation is the straight line method but again use an accountant or tax software to determine exact depreciation for each tax year. To determine depreciation one must know the cost basis for the property. Basis is what it cost to take ownership and place the property into operation.

Basis for the property can include many of the required fees to purchase the property as well as repairs required on the property to get it rent ready. Let's say an investor bought a property for a purchase price of $165000 but with closing costs and some repairs, the final cost to get renters in the door was $175000. $175000 can be used as the cost basis as long as everything is documented. This will be the starting point for calculating annual depreciation over the next 27.5 years.

Using this same example and the straight line method, for tax year 2019, this property could be depreciated $5727! The depreciation would be deducted from gross rental income for the property along with all other expenses, greatly reducing or perhaps even creating a loss on taxable rent income. As mentioned earlier, real estate owners may also depreciate major repairs and even tools required to keep the property maintained. This gets a little complicated to keep up with and yet again a reason to secure a good tax software program or accountant.

Depreciation is the best tax benefit of owning investment property but does come with a catch. When selling an investment property, the investor will have to pay capital gains taxes on the net profit based on the depreciated value of the property. For instance, if selling a property for a net price of $200,000 and it's been depreciated down to $120,000 for tax purposes, there will be capital gains tax on the $80,000 profit.

So isn't this a question of pay now or pay later? Well sort of. Think about the time value of money we discussed in the "invest early, invest often" chapter. Real estate is a long term investment. The growth of 20 years' worth of tax advantaged income from real estate that is wisely reinvested should outweigh any capital gains tax burden when the property is sold.

Also, there are many tax advantaged means to dispose of a real estate investment. A 1031 exchange rolls the proceeds from the sale of a property towards the purchase of a like kind investment thus avoiding capital gains tax. Currently, passing on an investment property as part of an estate will also mitigate the capital gains if the heirs choose to sell the property. Regardless, even with paying capital gains tax upon sale of an investment property, the tax advantages to owning real estate in the here and now are substantial.

So what does all this look like in practice? Generally speaking, after all the aforementioned expenses are deducted from our gross rental income, our *taxable rental income* is about 50% less than what we actually net! Don't leave money on the table by not understanding rental income tax advantages! For the last time (at least in this section), seek help from professionals as necessary to understand this important part of real estate investments income stream.

TIP #20: Investing in real estate is a people business; know tenants well

My assumption is many folks steer clear of real estate investing because it is inherently a people business. From working with a real estate agent while searching for the right property to the loan officer at the bank to secure financing, owning real estate requires near constant interaction with fellow humans. Working with a bank or real estate agent is the easy part! As you probably guessed, the challenging people side of the rental property business is developing a relationship with tenants.

Although I served as a leader in the military for nearly a quarter century, on a Meyers Briggs personality type indicator I am a high performing introvert. It doesn't come natural for me to engage, persuade and sometimes confront other people. Unfortunately, my wife is exactly the same.

That being said, we've learned over the years how to communicate effectively with tenants, from the moment they arrive as a prospect, to the time they move out. There is really no secret to good tenant – landlord relations. First and foremost, treat everyone with dignity and respect. My wife and I pride ourselves on offering clean, well maintained and affordable rental homes. She does the showing, lease paperwork and day to day management while I work maintenance and repair issues. We both interact with our tenants with courtesy and professionalism. "Yes ma'am / No sir" are the norms. And guess what? Our tenants mirror that behavior right back at us!

But alas I am getting ahead of myself! How do you get the right tenant? Well like most things there is always a measure of risk involved. While we treat our tenants with dignity and respect, we screen and vet everyone! This starts during showing of the unit. My wife will voice verify prospects prior to making an appointment to show the property. During the appointment, she follows basic security rules such as checking in / out, remaining between the prospects and the exit door as well as other common sense measures.

Once a prospective tenant is interested in a property, we use both a standard rental application as well as a tenant screening service offered by one of the major credit reporting companies. The prospective tenant pays for the screening service as part of the application fee and the results include a credit, criminal and eviction history check. The screening service even provides a "decline" or "accept" recommendation! I highly recommend the use of one of these services.

Often there will be numerous prospective tenants who meet the "accept" threshold. It's always tough but we contact each applicant and let them know their status. We have to choose the best qualified applicant based on their screening score. Once a candidate is selected, we go back to the traditional application to verify current residence and employment. The selection process takes time but is probably the most critical step of owning and renting properties. Fortunately, we've gotten it correct more than we've gotten it wrong!

So now we've got a new tenant, what's next? The easiest way to summarize this aspect of rental property management is, life happens. Air conditioners will break, typically on the hottest day of the year. Pipes will begin leaking on Saturday night. Key to keeping tenants content is to respond quickly to every maintenance request. For the easy stuff, I will take care of the problem as soon as I leave my day job or on the weekend. For the bigger issues, we have a list of service providers that usually respond quickly. Tenants are essentially paying landlords for a service they do not wish to handle themselves, maintain the residence.

What about a tenant that is slow to pay or can't pay rent? Despite the best screening efforts, as I mentioned in the paragraph above, life happens. Tenants may lose a job or as we've seen this year, there may be a global pandemic. Again, dignity and respect with a mix of firmness will take the day. First and foremost, ensure a good understanding of the laws in the state which the property is located. Most are pretty straight forward and spell out tenant as well as landlord rights during the eviction process.

Tenants don't want to get evicted and while we have encountered some habitual slow payers, who seem willing to pay our $50 late fee frequently, we've only experienced a couple of renters who got in a situation where they absolutely could not pay rent. In these cases, we explain in clear terms the eviction process and help them understand that an eviction is a court ordered judgement that will follow them around for years and may hinder their ability to secure quality housing in the future. In each case, they have chosen to just abandon the premises rather than face the eviction process. While we lost a little money on these cases, the unit is cleared and we can turn the property for a new renter relatively quickly. In my opinion, this is a better option than going through the sometimes lengthy court process.

A quick word on tenants that may not be living up to the terms of the lease agreement. This could include subletting the property, not performing tenant required maintenance or just keeping the property in an unclean or unsafe condition. Again, check local laws first but we've found most people respond well to firm but fair communications. Show them the paragraph in their signed, legally binding contract where they agreed not to exhibit the bad behaviors. Remind them that a breach of this contract could be grounds for an eviction process and all the negative aspects that come with it. We've found most folks will comply.

The big takeaways from this tip, use a screening process, know the local laws (reflect them in your lease) and treat people with respect. Establishing a good relationship with your tenants and being a landlord is not really a scary proposition at all. We've been fortunate to have some great tenants who we still keep in contact with after they move out into their own home!

TIP #21: Cover your assets

Probably a close second reason many people choose to not plunge into real estate investing is the very real risk that comes with owning property. What if the property burns down or is otherwise damaged? What if a tenant or their guest is injured at the property? Valid concerns but fortunately there are several means to protect ones interests from these infrequent occurrences. In thirteen years in the real estate business, we've had a few issues. I'll go over some ways to "cover your assets" and relate some of our scar tissue. Again, this is yet another area where more self-study is required to determine the best coverage plan for your personal situation.

Most insurance companies offer rental property homeowners insurance that will offer the coverages required by not only the mortgage lender, but also state law. An owner can dial up or dial down coverages, deductibles and other features of these policies but with every change comes an associated cost in premiums. We choose to keep fairly high deductibles on our policies and only go with the minimum required coverages by law in order to keep annual premiums low. For the states where we own property, this includes rebuild cost in the case of a total loss as well as liability coverage for injury to tenants.

An important note, rental property homeowner's policies do not cover contents of the property. It is very important to explain this to tenants in the lease and highly recommend they secure a renters policy for the residence. One feature rental property homeowner's policies do include that is a nice is lost rent coverage. Ensure a good understanding of rental property policy coverages and cost. Don't over insure but absolutely do not under insure either. Work with an insurance agency you trust to determine the right policy for the circumstances.

We have filed claims on our rental property homeowner's insurance policy twice. While both of these events caused some stress, in the long term, we came out on top and even increased the value of our properties! Our first claim was for a roof on one of our slightly older duplexes. It was beginning to have recurring leaks and a wind storm pretty much finished it off. This also was one of our out of state properties managed by a property manager.

Working with our insurance company and property management team, we were able to get a better, longer lasting, more attractive roof installed and we only paid the deductible on our policy. The deductible was able to be written off our taxes and the new roof certainly added value to the property. This process is pretty much automatic for the insurance companies and it went fairly smooth.

For the other claim we weren't quite as lucky. One of our top floor condo units developed a leak in the water supply to the dishwasher and the tenant didn't report it until several hours later. I will go into much more detail on this episode in the "be diligent" truth chapter as there are some great teaching points. I would estimate at least twenty to thirty gallons of water leaked into our unit's kitchen and the ceilings of the condo units below.

Needless to say, this was a heck of a mess and there was a lot of water damage! While my insurance company was fairly responsive, they also took a hard stance that ended up costing me some out of pocket expense. They would not cover damages to our neighbors units as upon their investigation, the insurance company determined no negligence on our part caused the leak.

Despite the insurance company's determination, it was water from my unit's pipes that damaged my neighbor's property and I felt obligated to make good with them. We settled up on our own and I paid one owner's insurance deductible and paid for the other owner's repairs. Fortunately, our insurance company came through on repairs to our condo unit. They also paid lost rent as we had to refund some of our tenant's rent while she stayed with friends during repairs.

That being said, repairing our condo unit wasn't exactly easy. The insurance company pledged to provide $10000 to make needed repairs to the appliances, kitchen cabinets and flooring. Not knowing any better, I called a general contractor to come take a look at the job. When he arrived he laughed out loud. He said he wouldn't even touch the job for anything less than $30000!

I thought this was a little ridiculous but suspected I'd get the same story from other general contractors. So, I did it myself! To be fair, I really just did the contracting, not all of the actual work. I used a handyman I knew to do the drywall, trim and paint. A budget flooring store replaced the sub flooring and floor coverings. Lastly, I had a big box store take care of the cabinets, counter tops and appliances.

We had a 100% new remodeled kitchen with stainless steel appliances, new cabinets, granite countertops and new flooring for $10000! These improvements instantly built equity in our condo unit and made the place look awesome. While we did have to come out of pocket some on this challenging experience, all in all we came out on top. When life gives you lemons, make lemonade!

If these two vignettes do not illustrate the importance of maintaining a good homeowner's policy on real estate investment properties, then I don't know what will! Still, there are additional measures one can take to cover assets.

Real estate that lies in a flood plain will require flood insurance, especially if there is a mortgage on the property. Regular rental property homeowner's policies do not cover flood damage. Flood insurance premiums are set by the government and expensive. Additionally, FEMA flood maps are often changing but are readily available on line to determine if a property lies within a flood plain. Always complete due diligence regarding flood plains as I am about to share some of our scar tissue on the topic! Generally, I'd recommend not purchasing investment properties in flood plains, but sometimes it cannot be helped due to very conservative flood area designations made by FEMA in the post hurricane Katrina era.

We purchased a property in central Texas that sat next to a bone dry drainage creek. During the closing process, both the appraisal as well as the bank's flood certification came back indicating the property did not lie in a flood plain. About two weeks after closing, the bank notified us that the property did in fact lie within a flood plain and we would need to secure flood insurance.

Our lawyer contacted the bank with our concerns. We had well documented evidence that state licensed service providers secured by the bank and that we had paid for, indicated the property was not in a flood zone. Turns out, the appraiser and flood cert person were using outdated FEMA maps in their assessment! Long story short, we were able to work out a compromise with the bank to maintain a "force placed" flood policy on the property for only the amount of the mortgage, not the whole property and contents value which tremendously reduced the required premiums. While this increased our expenses for the property, it didn't cut into our profit margin terribly. The point of this little vignette is do *your own* due diligence anytime purchasing a property and take into consideration flood insurance requirements!

I didn't learn about umbrella insurance policies until later in life when our financial advisor suggested we consider additional protection for our assets. Umbrella policies simply add additional liability protection for exposures (think rental properties) above and beyond what is covered in a homeowners or auto policy. Important to note, for someone to sue for damages and win, they must first prove that there were in fact damages and that the damages were caused by negligence. That being said, a successful law suit could potentially claim damages that would far exceed the $300000 liability coverage on most auto or homeowners policies!

Umbrella policy coverage usually starts at $1 million and work their way up. Fortunately, annual premiums on umbrella policies are not terribly expensive considering the amount they cover. Within the policy, each exposure will be identified and includes properties owned as well as licensed drivers within the household. Once an investor's portfolio starts reaching into the hundreds of thousands or there are teenage drivers in the household, an umbrella policy can add an extra layer of protection for the assets we've worked so hard to attain!

Lastly, yet another means of covering your assets is to hold real estate investments within a Limited Liability Company or LLC for short. LLCs simply provide another layer of protection such that, in the event of a lawsuit, only the LLC's assets are potentially at risk, not personal assets.

There are pros and cons to establishing an LLC. There are fees required to establish an LLC and most likely you'll have to pay business privilege taxes to maintain the entity (all tax deductible by the way). Also, to title a property to an LLC, one will either need to purchase it with a business loan which has generally less favorable terms than a conventional mortgage or pay cash.

As you may recall in our financing tip, we used creative financing means to purchase our condo properties and therefore brought cash to closing. We were able to deed these properties in our LLC.

Some pros to establishing an LLC also include doing business as a business rather than as an individual. An LLC will enable the real estate investor to establish business bank accounts, business credit cards and generally do all business related manners in the name of the LLC rather than in the investor's own name. This adds that layer of separation between an investor and their business dealings. The best part is that for tax purposes, income generated from the LLC is just counted as regular individual income. No need to mess around with any of the confusing corporate tax mess!

We didn't establish an LLC until about eight years into our rental property investment adventure. Despite the additional (tax deductible) costs, it was a good move for us. I hope to someday have all of our properties deeded in the name of our LLC for an added layer of liability protection. Weigh the pros and cons to determine if establishing a LLC for additional protection is the right move.

Before closing the chapter on the "collect rent, don't pay it" financial truth, I want to review a few key points as I know we've covered a lot of ground here. Important to remember, real estate investments build wealth in three distinct ways 1. Rental income 2. Tax advantages 3. Building equity. All three of these work symbiotically to make real estate investments a unique position and an important part of every aspiring millionaire's portfolio.

Rental investing is a big commitment and requires sacrifice. It sometimes requires purchasing that first property later in life, after saving up capital and making purchases based on profitability, not emotion. It may mean delaying the purchase of that first single family home until the early 40s. Keep credit in good shape and look creatively at financing options when considering a real estate investment. Simply put, sacrifice and save during early earning years in order to afford that forever home in later years!

Location, location, location is more than just a cliché but an absolute truth when it comes to investing in real estate. We make money from real estate when we buy it. Do the market analysis for the area under consideration. Determine expected rental income and required expenses in order to determine capitalization rate for a potential property, 8-10% is the desired target.

Nothing about rental income is "passive", treat real estate investing like a part time job or side hustle and it will help keep your mind right for all the ups and downs. Learn to do it yourself as much as possible. Managing expenses is critical to staying profitable with real estate investing.

Don't leave money on the table come tax time. Use the tax advantages of rental property ownership as another income stream. Seek help, smart tax moves is one area where we definitely need a professional. Reinvest your profits and let them compound!

Lastly, real estate investment is an inherently people business from day one. Learn to get comfortable communicating and negotiating with bankers, real estate agents as well as tenants. Treat tenants with dignity and respect but vet thoroughly using a screening service. Respond to maintenance issues quickly, do not defer. Because real estate investment is a people business, an investor must cover their assets. Homeowner's insurance is a must and there are several other ways to add additional layers of protection from risk.

I read articles almost daily about formulas for building a million dollar net worth by investing aggressively in stocks or mutual funds. This approach to millionaire status ignores what I believe to be a financial truth, owning real estate and not paying rent is essential to build wealth. Many would argue the juice is not worth the squeeze but I will gladly take on that argument. I do not believe a worker can get to a million dollar net worth on mutual fund investments alone and especially if paying someone like me rent every month.

I covered a lot of information in this chapter with the hope to alleviate some common fears and misperceptions about real estate investing. Hopefully my own experiences with real estate investing, both positive and negative, will help inspire a lifelong commitment to this financial truth. One final word of warning, real estate investing is addictive! Closing on a new property and securing a signed lease from a tenant is an incredibly rewarding feeling. Most folks that really get into it will immediately start looking for their next property! Just remember, real estate is but one of five truths on the journey to becoming a millionaire.

Now let's check in on the financial review of our notional subject's journey towards millionaire status!

Truths in Action Financial Review #3 (Ages 30-34)

Highlights: 20% withholding and income taxes beginning at age 30. Child #2 at age 30. Payoff 2nd car at age 33. Raise in compensation and buy another duplex at 33 ($37000 sold from taxable investment, $152000 financed at 4% for 30 years), "comfortable" benchmark reached at 34.

	Yearly Income and Expenses Age 30-34					
	Age	30	31	32	33	34
Income	Annual Pre Tax Income	71114	72180	73264	83419	84670
	Gross Rental Income Property #1	10800	10800	10800	16800	22200
	Gross Rental Income Property #2				5700	11400
Invest	401K (employee contr.)	12000	12000	12000	18000	20000 (max)
	Taxable Investment	5000	5000	5000	10000	10000
	Child #1 529 plan	600	600	1200	1200	1200
	Child #2 529 plan	300	600	600	600	600
Expenses (Out)	Taxes / Withholding	14223	14436	14653	16684	16934
	Health & Dental Insurance	4200	4300	4400	4400	4500
	Mortgage #1 (Principle, Interest, tax, insurance)	14400	14400	15000	15000	15500
	Mortgage #2 (Principle, Interest, tax, insurance				6600	13200
	Home repairs and upkeep	1200	1200	1200	2400	2400
	Car 1 & 2 (payment, ins, gas, & maintenance)	8000	8000	8200	3500	3500
	Cell Phone and Utilities	4000	4000	4200	4200	4400
	Food	8000	9000	9000	10000	10000
	Remaining for Everything Else*	9991 (833/mo)	9444 (787/mo)	8611 (717mo)	13335 (1111/mo)	16036 (1336/mo)

*Everything else includes clothing, entertainment, other needs and building small surplus in checking.

Investments Summary

Compounded at 5% annually	Value at age 34
401K (+50% employer match)	177618
Child #1 529 Plan	7560
Offspring #2 529 Plan	3100
Taxable Investment ($37K withdraw at 33)	15157
Total Investment Accounts	203435

Property #1 Purchased age 29	
Value at purchase	190000
Down payment	10000
Principle paid to age 34	159133
Value age 35 (Appreciation)	226870 (+36870)
Total Real Estate Net Equity	67737

Property #2 Purchased age 33	
Value at purchase	190000
Down payment	38000
Principle remaining at age 34	147009
Value age 34 (3% / Yr Appreciation)	201571 (+11571)
Total Real Estate Net Equity	54562

Net worth at age 34: $325734

Chapter 5: Truth #4 - Be Diligent

Americans are traditionally known as a hardworking people. Many Americans define themselves by the work they do and most strive to do their best on the job. Whether it is out of necessity or for love of their profession, Americans are some of the hardest working folks on the planet. I would not dare insult a reader of this book by insinuating they didn't fit this description!

The "be diligent" truth is not meant to imply the absence of hard work, but rather in this context, diligence is a quality that should complement working hard. Oxford defines diligent as "having or showing care and conscientiousness in one's work or duties." As it applies to financial truths, being diligent is really a frame of mind for our everyday lives, the "duties" if you will, of being a good worker, investor, spouse, parent or citizen.

Perhaps I am letting my military background show by placing a premium on the "be diligent" truth. Diligence is certainly a well-respected attribute in military circles. Those Soldiers who are able to clue in on a situation, perform tasks to standard or better yet work proactively, are well respected and duly rewarded. One of the most common and age old military duties of "police call" or in civilian terms, walking through an area and picking up trash, is actually designed to train Soldiers to recognize things that don't belong. I believe this same behavior is desirable in our personal lives. We must continually strive to be diligent in every task which usually means recognizing those things that don't belong or are broken. This is what makes diligence an absolutely necessary truth on the path to becoming a millionaire on a worker's budget.

So what does diligence look like in our day to day lives? First it's best to describe what diligence is not. If American's value working hard, we also value playing hard and our leisure time. Many American's, myself included, were raised where after dinner, it was time to plop down in front of the TV and channel surf until we find a show that caught our attention. Today, it is probably more like staring at the smart phone or perhaps banging away on the gaming console for hours on end.

Similarly, many of us will sleep in on the weekends. And when I say sleep in, I am talking until noon! Some of this is out of physiological necessity. How could we be expected to get up early on the weekend if watching TV or gaming until 4 a.m. the previous night?

Lastly, we all procrastinate. How many of us wait until the due date to pay bills? Going back to rental properties for a moment, if a landlord puts in a lease that rent is due on the 1st and late after the 5th, guess when they will receive the rent check? Yep, 99% of the time on the 5th.

The behaviors I've just described are the antithesis of being diligent. It is a safe assumption that very successful people are diligent and do not exhibit the aforementioned behaviors on a routine basis. Does this mean we need to throw away the TV and wake up at 6am on Saturday's? No not always, but it does mean that we need to show "care and consciousness" in our personal and financial lives, *all the time*.

Let's look at how these basic examples of diligence might play out in our daily lives. First bill paying. Why wait to the last minute and introduce risk into what is already a stressful activity? Too often, our payment gets lost in the mail or an electronic payment is fat fingered incorrectly causing us to be late on the payment. This could have negative impacts on credit reporting and our overall financial goals.

I would submit the diligent person has figured out how to keep a surplus in their checking account to be able to pay bills immediately upon receipt and does so *every month*. I certainly understand many Americans must wait until payday to pay bills but I firmly believe that for even those of us on the tightest budgets, one can build up enough surplus in a checking account to enable paying bills on receipt.

What about the TV watching and gaming, what's the harm in that? Nothing if done in moderation, just like any habit. How many times have I already mentioned about self-study in this book? Replace that TV or game time with internet research on investment products or tax code. Better yet, sign up for a night course in a particular financial topic. How do successful people spend their down time?

My kids always give me a ton of crap about smartphone time in the evenings. True enough, from their perspective it appears I spend too much time on the phone and computer. I then show them what I am reading, usually either information regarding our current financial status or researching the next big financial move.

Does this mean fill every waking moment researching, planning and educating about our financial future? Absolutely not! Balance is important to maintaining our sanity and if we don't disengage from time to time, we may become myopic in our vision. As much as I love planning finances, if I focused on it 24/7 I'd quickly lose perspective of what really matters in life, my family. I freely admit I've struggled with balance over the years in my professional and personal life. While our family has achieved success, there are times I regret not focusing more on just being a good dad or husband. Life isn't a dressed rehearsal and you can't get those moments back.

Which brings me to an important point. Being diligent as a financial truth goes well beyond just paying bills on time and spending free time working on personal finances. Diligence is a way of life that can best be described as fixing what's broken, not later, but right now. While this chapter will talk in terms of the material, the diligence truth certainly applies to people and relationships as well! The metaphors will be apparent as we go along.

Too often we put our blinders on in life and walk right past something (or someone) we know is broken. When we see those shingles on our roof that have peeled back and will inevitably leak during the next big rainstorm, we usually just keep on trucking and don't stop immediately to call a roofer. How many faucets with the tiniest of leaks have we ignored? What about when we hear "no" from the banker / employer / partner? Do we immediately start figuring out how to get them to "yes"?

I've found these little "leaks" in life more often than not turn into big, expensive problems when ignored. The diligent thing to do is to stop and make repairs immediately. This truth applies on so many levels!

So why not just call this truth, "be attentive" or "be aware"? Diligent is the correct quality due to its connection to work and duties. In order to be aware of what's broken, you have to know what to look for! This truth requires constant practice. To become diligent one must gain knowledge, which as we will examine next chapter, takes a lifelong dedication to learning. Interesting how these five financial truths are all interrelated and complementing!

I asserted in the previous chapter, it will be challenging for a worker to build a net worth of a million dollars without owning real estate. It will be similarly challenging if the same worker isn't diligent in every aspect of their lives. A worker can volunteer for all the overtime and double shifts available. They may very well make a stack of money over time! But if the worker regularly walks past things in their life that are broken, there will always be "leaks" funneling wealth away. It will be very difficult to truly get ahead financially or emotionally.

I've only got three tips in this chapter but they are important ones. I hope the tips and corresponding examples illustrate how diligence is a truth we must embrace in order to build wealth. And, although it's certainly outside the scope of this book, hopefully these principles can help other aspects of your life as well.

Fortunately, owning real estate has given me tremendous insight on what it means to be diligent. Let's start out with a tip on a very practical and easy to understand application of diligence!

TIP #22: Never walk past a problem

Wait, you already said that! Please allow me to put a finer point on this tip and provide some examples of when I walked past problems that turned in to big, expensive headaches. Real estate investing and rental property management provide the maximum opportunity to practice diligence as there are problems encountered near daily. I want to share two stories that illustrate how not being diligent ended up costing time and money. If I had just been more diligent when I encountered a problem!

In 2016 we found an excellent for sale by owner duplex at a great price. While there were some evident issues that would need to be addressed, at that price point, it was just too good of a deal to pass up. The most serious problem I noticed on the property was the location of the water meters. For whatever reason, the builders had placed the meters almost in the middle of the asphalt parking area with the water supplies to the units running under the asphalt.

It doesn't take an engineer to realize that vehicle traffic continually running over and sometimes parking on top of the concrete casements surrounding the water meters would put pressure on the PVC water supply lines and they would eventually crack. There was even visual evidence where a failure had already occurred and the lines had to be dug up, repaired and then the parking area repaved.

The obvious quick fix would have been to relocate the meters in a grassy area off the parking lot and reroute the water supply lines back into the building where they were not under asphalt and constantly exposed to vehicular traffic. This would take some time and a few thousand dollars to repair but overall, not the most complex job for skilled workers.

Of course, the point of this vignette is to illustrate how not being diligent costs time and money! For whatever reason (really no good excuse), I didn't make the required repairs after we closed on the property. Not six months later I got the call, on a long, Memorial Day weekend of course, that water was pooling up in the parking area. Sure enough, the water line was cracked at the meter due to the constant strain from vehicles driving over it!

Nothing better than a Memorial Day weekend spent busting asphalt with a pick axe and covered in mud to focus the mind! A handy man friend of mine helped me dig up, fix and re asphalt the water line on the cheap but I had blown a whole weekend and spent about $500. Worse yet, we had only made a temporary fix, the problem wasn't resolved. A few months later I forked out the $3000 and assembled the help I needed to fix the problem properly. Haven't had to worry about it again.

You'd think I would have learned my lesson but sometimes life lessons are hard earned. Just a couple of years later another example of my non-diligence would prove even more catastrophic. I already shared a little about the massive water leak that occurred in one of our condo investment properties. A water supply line from the kitchen sink valve to the dishwasher popped loose leaking water at 50psi pressure for a number of hours resulting in significant water damage to our condo unit and the two units below. Here is the rest of the story....

This was our seventh real estate investment property and I thought I was a master investor! This condo was pretty small and I thought I knew enough about home inspections to forego paying a licensed inspector $350 to check out all aspects of the home. During my do-it-yourself pre-closing inspection, I noted some of the plumbing looked outdated and questionable. Especially the dishwasher supply line which was simply plastic tubing held onto the valve by a compression fitting. This is not up to current plumbing code as most water supplies under pressure require a hammer arrestor at the valve and a steel braided or otherwise more heavy duty line. Common sense dictated that a good bump of this plastic tubing would probably cause it to pop loose and leak water everywhere.

Of course, I walked right past the problem and it cost me dearly. Would I have made repairs to this item if discovered and reported by a licensed inspector? Probably not. I was too focused on closing the deal and getting a tenant into the residence instead of being diligent and fixing discovered problems. Even though my gut told me take action, I was not diligent.

The fallout from this leak episode took over two months to fully remediate. As I mentioned in the previous chapter, we came out of pocket $4000 to keep the peace with our neighbors. Working with our insurance company was a near daily battle but fortunately I was able to turn lemons into lemonade with the settlement and install a very nice, new kitchen on the cheap. That was most likely luck and timing than skill. I just happened to catch the materials on sale at the big box and was able to sub contract the repairs myself.

More impactful was the incredible stress placed on my family as well as our tenant during these two months. Thankfully our tenant was very understanding when she and her children had to move out for a few weeks while we made repairs. She did not have a renter's insurance policy and was not compensated for some of her damaged personal items. She was very pleased with the new kitchen when she moved back in.

This leak episode played out at the exact time I was transitioning from my career in the Army. On a positive note, I wasn't exactly taxed with duties in my day job as I was out processing from service. If this had occurred while my career was in full swing, I don't know how I would have handled it! On the downside, I spent numerous hours each day dealing with cleaning up a rental property mess instead of focusing on transitioning to a new chapter in my life. Additionally, our family had planned a big vacation overseas with extended family to celebrate retiring from 24 years of military service. Unfortunately, I was dealing with insurance adjusters and contractors while 5000 miles from home and in a different time zone at the expense of my family.

I walked past what appeared to be a small problem and it cost me in time, stress and money. While I used two vignettes from our real estate side hustle to exemplify non-diligence, there have been countless other times when I saw something wrong and didn't act. How many times have we seen that oil collecting around the valve covers on our car's engine or even dripping down onto the driveway or garage but just ignored it? What about those shingles that are flapping around or missing on the roof?

On a personal level, how many times have we seen a coworker, friend or loved one who was visibly having a problem but didn't stop to ask how we could help? These examples are all fairly evident, but many of life's problems are not. Trust your gut, when you see *or feel* there is a problem, immediately develop a plan to remediate. That is the essence of being diligent. Life's "leaks" can cost dearly and the non-diligent person will struggle to overcome these challenges on the road to becoming a millionaire.

TIP #23: Find a way to get to yes or go in a different direction

How often have we heard "no" from a loan application, job interview or any other request and just walked away. Perhaps even more relatable, how many times have we heard "yes" but not necessarily on the terms we were hoping for but just accepted it? The diligent response is to re-attack! Perform an analysis on what is causing the less than favorable response and correct the issue or in some cases go in a different direction, but above all never stop fighting. The diligent person, and thusly the millionaire worker, can't give up when they hear "no".

Like many of the tips in this book, getting to yes is easier said than done. Oftentimes we've put a lot of effort into our proposal and when we hear no, we may feel completely defeated. It is perfectly normal to want to give up. But consider the other persons perspective, "no" is a lot easier than "yes". There is less risk and no is always the safe bet. More often than not, we all default to "no" unless we have compelling evidence on why we should say yes. A diligent person recognizes this and will master the art of changing a default "no" response to a "yes".

Which brings us to the essence of getting to yes. First, ensure there is a clear understanding of the root cause for the response, then make required changes. For formal considerations such as a loan application, the lender will usually spell out reasons for disapproval. While the reasons may be challenging to overcome, such as a low credit score, the remedy is clear, improve the credit score. It is at this point the diligent person will commit to developing and executing a course of action to implement a fix. It may take some time, but do what it takes *now* to overcome what is causing the no.

Still another option is to go find a yes. Using the loan example, more likely than not, the next lender will probably still be a no. That being said, it is always prudent to get a second opinion when receiving a no. Every business conducts operations a little differently and follows differing business practices.

After our fourth mortgage for an investment property, we encountered an issue with our preferred lender while trying to acquire a fifth loan for another duplex. Due to certain regulatory guidance, this particular lender could not approve an individual for more than four mortgages. Dang, our dreams of building a real estate empire were over! Not so fast. After calling around, I learned not all lenders follow the same regulatory guidance. One bank responded, "we will approve as many loans as you qualify for"! We established a relationship with this bank and haven't looked back. They just recently refinanced our home! If I had given up on the first no, we wouldn't have pursued our last three duplexes and our net worth wouldn't be near where it is now!

Lastly, getting to yes may mean re-attacking at a different time or going in a completely different direction. The diligent person can recognize quickly when they won't make it to yes on a particular endeavor and will develop a plan to change directions immediately. Early in my Army career I was afforded an opportunity to earn a Master's degree in counseling. I also completed the additional supervision and testing requirements to earn certification as a Nationally Certified Counselor (NCC). While pursuing the certification, my understanding was that the NCC certification carried reciprocity with most states' counseling licensure requirements.

My initial retire from the military plan was to convert my NCC to a Licensed Professional Counselor (LPC) license for whatever state we landed in and continue to serve by counseling those in need of help. About a year out from retirement, I started working with the counseling licensing board in my state.

Needless to say the application and professional endorsement requirements are quite lengthy and it had been 15 years since I completed my graduate course work. It took several months to put together the application packet but I finally mailed it off and anxiously awaited my shiny new counselor license in the mail.

What I received instead was a tersely worded, five page single spaced letter from the president of the board on why my packet was insufficient to grant licensure. Pretty tough pill to swallow for someone who, at least in my professional life, hadn't heard "no" very frequently. This started three months of back and forth with me pleading the case that my academic and professional experience met licensure requirements.

The outcome, the licensing board was unmoved. They wanted me to go back to school for additional training which would have taken well over a year. I was retiring in about six months at this point and needed a job!

After much deliberation, I decided to go in a completely different direction. Although I think I had a lot to offer as a 24 year military veteran and a school trained counselor, I couldn't get the state board to yes. It just wasn't in the best interest for my family to take a year off from work for additional schooling. Perhaps seeking a counselor license will be my next career!

I shifted gears and decided to follow the path of many veterans and seek employment within the defense industry. I immediately set to work building my resume and networking to that end. Long story short, I landed an excellent job which pays much better than a counselor would have, albeit maybe not as personally rewarding. The point of this vignette is don't be afraid to change directions when overcoming a "no" is too big of a hill to climb.

Whether buckling down to fix what is causing the no, seeking another option that will result in a yes or changing directions completely, the whole point of this tip is to take action! The diligent person will not receive a no and stop, they will immediately figure out an alternate course of action.

TIP #24: Always be on time and stop procrastinating

Diligent people are always punctual in every aspect of their lives. In the military, we had a saying, "to be on time is to be ten minutes early". I am actually glad to no longer feel beholden to that mantra, but like most things in the military there is superb utility to the idea. Procrastination and putting things off to the last minute it the antithesis of diligence. Being diligent is so much more than paying bills prior to the due date and being punctual. More accurately, the diligent person is present at the *decisive time* and in the *decisive place* to influence outcomes.

But being diligent and always on time starts with the basics. Can't stress enough to never be late on payments. To be honest, I didn't realize how much visibility a late payment gets until we started using a credit service to screen our tenants.

When we pull our prospective tenant's report, we are able to see every payment they've made on every instance of revolving debt over the past several years! The report identifies whether the payments were 30, 60 or 90 days late.

What difference does it make as long as they payed? If you recall from the last chapter, oftentimes there are several prospective tenants determined as qualified by the screening service. When it comes to a tie breaker, we start looking at which tenant has the best history of on time payments. The one who shows a history of paying on time, wins. I suspect we are not the only landlords who process tenant screening reports in this manner and I think it's a safe bet mortgage and auto lenders assess payment history similarly.

It also blows my mind when we have tenants who habitually pay rent after the five day grace period and tack on the $50 late fee. We aren't the only ones who charge late fees! Paying late fees are like speeding tickets, just pouring money away. Definitely not diligent behavior and not conducive to growing a million dollar net worth on a worker's budget.

Let's talk for a moment about being on time in the truest sense of the word. As a leader and manager over the past quarter century, nothing drove me more crazy than untimeliness in the workplace. It's been my privilege to work with extremely intelligent and capable people over the years who can accomplish just about any task. But if they can't deliver the product by the suspense date, I assessed their performance behind peers who got good work in on time. It's not personal, just business.

Similarly, walking in late to a meeting is *always* duly noted despite what might be said flippantly as we walk through the door. Americans as a whole are getting more skilled in the workplace. If struggling with timeliness, one risks quickly falling behind the competition.

So how does one stay on time? Probably the best way is to keep a calendar using one of the many apps for smartphones or PCs. I found as I progressed in my professional career, if an event or suspense wasn't entered into my calendar, it didn't really exist! It requires diligence to keep the calendar up to date and meaningful, but a good calendar is a necessary tool for the aspiring millionaire.

Let's go back to what it really means for the diligent person to be on time, being present at the *decisive time* and *decisive place*. First, what does decisive mean? Again, by using the term decisive I am letting my military background show but it's such a useful word! Simply put, decisive is the point in time or location when a decision must be made in order to achieve a favorable outcome. Easy enough right? Well, it takes a whole lot of skill and experience to 1. Identify the decisive points in life and 2. Be prepared to make that favorable decision when you arrive at the decisive point.

It's important to point out there are not clear signs for these decisive points, but with the correct training, one can condition themselves to instinctively know when they occur. I mentioned last chapter that my wife and I both had the goal of investing in real estate and that we acquired our first investment property in 2008 when we were stationed at Fort Hood in Killeen, TX. Although I may have implied that this all occurred by chance, please allow me to offer the rest of the story.

Wanting to own real estate is not enough, it takes some serious analysis to go from vision to reality. There are several Army postings inside and outside the United States where it would have been near impossible for us to realize our goal of owning real estate. So early on, while still stationed in New York, where we definitely were not able to invest, I began diligently researching Army bases that had favorable real estate markets nearby.

Fort Hood, Texas came up at the top of the list. Central Texas has a lot to offer and in the early 2000s the area was starting to show signs of a boom. Prices were good and as I mentioned in the last chapter, Killeen zoned somewhat uniquely in that the city allows multi-family homes mixed in predominantly single family neighborhoods.

So as we left New York in 2007 to attend a required Army one year school in Fort Leavenworth, Kansas, we made a decision to start shaping our follow on assignment to land at Fort Hood, TX. Fortunately, we were able to influence the process and get orders for Texas! Before graduating from the training course in Kansas in 2008, we had already traveled to Killeen, picked out a duplex and closed on the home!

The rest is history but in case you forgot from the last chapter, we purchased two more duplexes during our nearly four year assignment to Fort Hood, Texas. Our three duplexes in Texas are proven performers and their values have increased tremendously since we've owned them.

My wife and I successfully recognized the decisive time and place for beginning our journey in real estate investing. Was this more luck than skill? Probably, but as the old saying goes you make your own luck. We started researching nearly two years early to determine the Army post most conducive to real estate investing. If we hadn't started early, acted decisively and shaped the process, we could have ended up anywhere and may not have been able to start our real estate journey.

A key aspect of diligence is to be on time. Not just in the literal sense of the word when paying bills or in our professional lives, but being on time at the decisive points on the road to build wealth. Learn how to recognize these important milestones and have the knowledge to act decisively.

Diligence as a truth to build wealth can be challenging to acquire because it's an intangible. It's an attribute that the successful worker should develop. Fortunately, most of us already have the ground work to be diligent as we probably describe ourselves as hard workers. Diligence is not the same as hard work but rather complements our work and makes the use of our time more efficient. Furthermore, when we espouse diligence as a truth it impacts not only our working and financial lives but every aspect of our personal lives and relationships.

The essence of diligence is fixing what's broke in our lives not next week, but right now. To do this we must condition ourselves to never walk past a problem. Think about all the times we've walked past something that was either obviously or intuitively wrong. Did it end up costing more to deal with the issue later down the road than if we had just addressed it immediately?

Diligent people don't take the first "no" and walk away, they immediately regroup and develop a plan to set the conditions for a "yes". This may take some hard work and discipline to remedy such as in the case of poor credit, but nothing in life is easy and a diligent person will thrive on the challenge! Diligent folks will get a second opinion and double down when they hear "no". Perhaps the old saying "where there is a will, there is a way" is appropriate in this context! Lastly, the diligent person will understand when getting to "yes" is just a bridge to far and will have the moral courage to change direction, sometimes drastically.

Timeliness is an intuitive part of being diligent but it goes so much further than just being punctual. That being said, if one can't pay bills on time or is habitually late, these challenges must be overcome to truly espouse the diligent truth. Beyond being timely, the diligent person must develop the skill to recognize the *decisive times* and *places* in their lives. These are points that require our decision in order to achieve a favorable outcome. Not only must we recognize these points but we must also equip ourselves with knowledge to make the correct decision. More on this in the next chapter "knowledge is money"!

Critics would probably argue that the behaviors and attributes I've described in this chapter are incorrectly assigned to the word diligent. Maybe so. But I believe the word diligent is so powerful! Who doesn't want to be known as a diligent person?

I also believe that diligence connection to work makes it the perfect descriptor for a financial truth. Most Americans can relate easily about what it means to work hard. But adding the qualifier "diligent" to hard work opens up new doors. Define diligence as you will, but I believe the three tips we have reviewed in this chapter do it justice! More importantly, I know firsthand how these tips worked in my life.

I can't guarantee being diligent alone will lead to a net worth of a million dollars but coupled with the other four financial truths, the probability certainly increases! Regardless, diligence is an important attribute that, even if it doesn't lead to a million dollar net worth, will surely bring more peace and contentment in our personal life.

Before moving on to our final truth "knowledge is money", let's check in with a financial review of our notional subject. Look how close we are getting to a million dollar net worth. At age 39 our subject is less than $300000 away! The time value of money is truly amazing. If flipping back and forth between the chapters to see how the financial reviews are stacking up, not to worry. In chapter seven, we'll do a recap and walk through the progression of our notional subject over the years.

Truths in Action Financial Review #4 (Ages 35-39)

Highlights: 401k contributions exceeds max deductible portion, remainder of contribution is after tax. Minor promotion at age 36 and a significant promotion at age 39 to senior management. Another car purchased at 35 (30000 at 0% for 5 years).

	Yearly Income and Expenses Age 35-39					
	Age	35	36	37	38	39
Income	Annual Pre Tax Income	85940	94786	96208	97651	115976
	Gross Rental Income Duplex #1	22200	22800	22800	23400	23400
	Gross Renal Income Duplex #2	11400	11700	11700	12000	12000
Invest	401K (employee contr. exceeds max tax deductible)	20000 (max)	21000	21000	22000	27000
	Taxable Investment	10000	10000	10000	10000	15000
	Child #1 529 plan	1200	1800	1800	1800	1800
	Child #2 529 plan	600	1200	1200	1200	1200
Expenses (Out)	Taxes / Withholding	17188	18957	19241	19530	23195
	Health & Dental Insurance	4500	4600	4600	4800	5000
	Mortgage #1 (Principle, Interest, tax, insurance)	15500	16000	16000	16500	16500
	Mortgage #2 (Principle, Interest, tax, insurance)	13200	14000	14000	14500	14500
	Home repairs and upkeep	2400	2400	2400	2400	2400
	Car 1 & 2 (payment, ins, gas, & maintenance)	9500	9500	10000	10000	10000
	Cell Phone and Utilities	4400	4500	4500	4600	4600
	Food	10000	11000	11000	12000	12000
	Remaining for Everything Else*	11052 (921/mo)	14329 (1194/mo)	14967 (1247/mo)	13721 (1143/mo)	18181 (1515/mo)

*Everything else includes clothing, entertainment, other needs and building small surplus in checking.

Investments Summary

Compounded at 5% annually	Value at age 39
401K (+50% employer match)	377281
Child #1 529 Plan	19326
Child #2 529 Plan	10152
Taxable Investment	82614
Total Investment Accounts	489373

Property #1 Purchased age 29	
Basis / Value at purchase	190000
Down payment	10000
Principle remaining age 39	137118
Value age 39 (3% Appreciation)	255344 (+65344)
Total Real Estate Net Equity	118226

Property #2 Purchased age 33	
Basis / Value at purchase	190000
Down payment	38000
Principle balance at age 39	131386
Value age 39 (Appreciation)	233676 (+43676)
Total Real Estate Net Equity	102290

Net worth at age 39: $709889

Chapter 6: Truth #5 - Knowledge is Money

Growing up, I witnessed first-hand the value of an education, or more accurately, the struggle required to be successful without an education. My immediate family, mother, father, stepfather and grandparents were working class folk. None of them had a college degree or any specialized certifications. They all worked very hard and eventually, earned respectable livings. My mother worked all the way until she was 67 and in her later years, when she wasn't at work, took care of my ill stepfather before he passed. She really didn't have a choice.

I hold the deepest respect for my hard working family. Their example taught me about working hard and saving money as well as set the foundation for the success my own family is enjoying today. My parents continually stressed the importance of an education. They didn't specify what that meant, most likely they didn't really know. They didn't have the same opportunities I had to seek formal education beyond high school. Unfortunately, since I grew up in the pre-529 era, they weren't able to save much for my post high school education either.

But they continually emphasized the importance. They knew if I didn't get an education, I'd have to scratch out a living the best I could like they did. I understood clearly their point, there has got to be a better way!

In fact, today it is almost impossible to earn a living the way my family did and the probability of becoming a millionaire without some type of formal education or certification is even less. With more and more workers acquiring specialized skills as well as many jobs being replaced by automation, opportunities for unskilled, high school graduates are constantly decreasing. It doesn't mean an unskilled laborer can't find a job, it just means the opportunity for upward mobility and increased income is much lower, even lower than it was just a few decades ago when my parents were working.

Which brings us to our final truth, knowledge is money. If you don't have knowledge, get some! Seek knowledge all the time and never stop. And yes, I am talking about knowledge in every sense of the word. From college degrees, to licenses, certifications and everything in between. My experience has taught me that without a lifelong pursuit of knowledge, becoming a millionaire on a workers budget will be a tough, if not impossible fight. While this is the last truth in the book, this was the first financial truth I learned many decades ago.

As if I needed more convincing about the importance of an education, when I entered college and joined Army ROTC, the military showed me first-hand how it values education and training. For those unfamiliar with the military, commissioned officers are required to earn a Bachelor's degree before or shortly after commissioning. Commissioned officers are typically brought into the Army via one of three sources, the United States Military Academy, Officer Candidate School, or the Reserve Officer Training Corps.

After completing the program of instruction at one of these three commissioning sources and a bachelor's degree, the officer is commissioned a Second Lieutenant. They are placed in charge of a platoon sized organization, usually around 40 people. Yes, a college degree and a few years training is all it takes to be a manager and leader of 40 people!

Of course within this organization are seasoned Non-commissioned Officers or NCOs for short, who rose through the ranks and possess from four to fifteen years' experience. They also have received extensive leadership training albeit a little different from the leadership training officers receive. Yet these extremely skilled and talented leaders, who oftentimes also possess college degrees, are not ultimately in charge. Furthermore, the NCOs salary, which is a matter of public record if interested, is proportionally much less, than the young 23 year old commissioned officer fresh out of college.

When I first entered the Army, I was a bit disillusioned by this disparity. After witnessing my parent's example, I naively thought more work equaled more pay. But I soon realized the Army served as an excellent cross section of society and this was the real world.

The Army places a premium on education and is pretty straight forward about it. Fortunately, the military over the past 20 or so years has done a lot to recognize the immense talent within the ranks and shore up some of the pay gap between officer and enlisted personnel. Yet the chasm is still present and like many things, it mirrors our American society. Recall, we used the 2020 enlisted military pay charts as the basis for income within our financial reviews.

I was also able to see the premium placed on education when I rejoined the civilian workforce almost two years ago. As a 24 year Army officer veteran, my executive level leadership experience and education, although somewhat narrowly focused, was immense. After networking, applying and interviewing, I was fortunate to land a great job as a middle level manager at a well-respected defense industry company. I was amazed at the benefits and compensation package.

But as I've reintegrated into the civilian workforce, I've noticed, like the military, there is a premium on education and credentials. Most of the senior management and executive level leaders are younger than me. Generally speaking, they earned their position by attaining multiple advanced degrees and certifications from well-respected schools coupled with about a decade of superb on the job performance. They've worked hard to climb the corporate ladder and needless to say, their compensation matches their achievements.

Compared to a Lieutenant Colonel or Colonel who serves as an executive level military leader, these civilian leaders do much better salary wise! Don't get me wrong, I don't have one iota of regret for the path I chose. In fact, I firmly believe it was my successful career in the Army that enabled me to even enter this part of our working society. I wouldn't change a thing. But it drives home the truth my working class parents taught me decades ago. Education and training are critical to success and building wealth.

You may have noticed in the financial reviews an assumption I made about our notional subject is they are regularly promoted to positions of increased responsibility and higher compensation. This assumes the subject is continually seeking knowledge, education and self-improvement. If he or she simply attempted to remain a hardworking, unskilled laborer, then the assumptions I've made about compensation are invalid. Workers must continually seek knowledge regardless of how proficient they are in job performance.

How many times have we seen this play out in our workplace? The retail worker who may be the best in their department for years but never sought any additional training or education is quickly passed by someone with less experience but better credentials. The skilled laborer, let's say a welder, who does not seek additional training and skillsets beyond basic welding will not advance in their profession. The same holds true for plumbers, electricians and other skilled workers.

While nirvana for most of us is to one day become self-employed and tell our bosses to take this job and shove it, the truth is, most of us will need to rely on employment as our primary source of income. A further truth is we will find it hard to incrementally earn more at work and subsequently build wealth if we remain stagnant. If you are not a self-starter who continually seeks knowledge in order to advance, I highly recommend a period of self-reflection to determine how to embrace this important truth!

I've talked at length so far in this chapter about the direct cause and effect of the knowledge is money truth as it relates to potential advancement and higher wages in the work place. Let's take a look at a little less tangible aspect of this truth and examine how the pursuit of knowledge is important in other aspects of our financial lives.

If you take anything away from this book, it should be that working hard, earning a paycheck and saving like crazy will most likely not get a worker to a million dollar net worth. It takes fully espousing and living all the truths we've covered to include investing early and often, living frugally, investing in real estate, diligence and knowledge. The knowledge truth is unique in that, much like diligence, it is a personal attribute that complements all the other financial truths.

First, and perhaps backtracking just a bit, let's define knowledge. Knowledge is information acquired through education or experience. Although I've emphasized formal education in the first half of this chapter (and we will drill down even more in an upcoming tip), I want to clearly emphasize "knowledge is money" includes so much more.

How many times have I stressed, "research" or "self-study" on a particular topic within this book such as investing, real estate or taxes? At the risk of sounding boastful, my wife and I have built extremely successful mutual fund and real estate investment portfolios. Neither of us have taken one formal class on financial management or real estate. We just went out seeking knowledge from a variety of sources and educated ourselves.

So what does that mean exactly? In simplest terms, pursuing knowledge is gathering information from someone who knows. This can be a real life advisor or web based literature, but above all, the source must be reputable and accurate. In fact, the research to determine reputability and accuracy is just as important as finding the source of information itself! There should be numerous sources for each area in which you are expanding knowledge. Often we may receive conflicting information, this is perfect! We learn best by comparing and contrasting the information we receive, then making our own decisions as to which information is most useful for our purpose. This provides an important quality to the knowledge…ownership.

Self-study takes time and a near constant dedication, which we will dive deeper into in just a moment. In today's interconnected world, the web has made gathering multiple sources of information on a particular topic easy. That being said, I would recommend not relying entirely on the internet. Pick up a book, pick up the phone or meet an advisor in person but above all seek out information.

Another recurring point you've heard in this book is "do it yourself". You just won't be able to build wealth within your real estate portfolio quickly if you are paying an electrician or plumber to fix every little problem. Again at the risk of sounding boastful, I can fix pretty much any basic electrical or plumbing problem safely and on the cheap! And I am about one of the most non-mechanically inclined people you will ever meet. How did I gain this knowledge?

First and foremost, the internet is the do it yourselfer's playground. If you can't find a video on the internet that shows you how to perform just about any task, then there are plenty of great web articles that can walk even the most unhandy handyman through repair jobs. Obvious implied task here is having a smartphone good enough that, when you are wedged under a kitchen sink replacing a valve, you can see / hear the instructions!

Second, and this applies for pretty much all forms of knowledge, learn by doing. One story illustrates this very clearly and my dad reminds me of it all the time. On one snowy day at age 16 I was stuck at my dad's house due to school closure. He needed to replace the dishwasher in his kitchen and the new one was sitting in the middle of the floor while he was at work. Bored out of my mind, I thought I'd give dishwasher installation a go!

Mind you, this is pre internet days, but by being observant and looking at how the old dishwasher was connected as well as reading the enclosed instructions with the new one, I was able to install the dishwasher by myself which worked well for nearly 20 years!

When I do have to call in a repair person, I always follow them closely and watch what they are doing. Always ask first before shadowing a plumber or electrician, but most of them are eager to show off their craft. I have learned more about plumbing and electrical repair this way and saved untold repair costs!

As a side note, plumbers and electricians clearly recognize they will lose work if by watching them, a customer learns how to do it themselves, but I've found most would prefer this. Skilled workers had rather focus on the higher paying, big jobs rather than the smaller ones that suck up their time. Home inspections when purchasing real estate are similar. After watching about a half dozen home inspections, I realized the checks are not that difficult to perform and pretty intuitive. I do them myself on smaller properties.

Experience is the best teacher and yes there is some risk. A 110 volt live wire does get your attention when it arcs, but rest assured, you will only forget to turn off power at the breaker box once! The key to doing it yourself is move very slowly and deliberately. Calculate and understand each step. Do it yourself repair jobs will take two or three times longer than a pro, but it will save so much money. Eventually, after performing a repair several times, the do it yourselfer may even go as fast as a pro! To gain experience requires putting fears aside and just doing it.

Another important part of gaining knowledge is retaining information. Too often I've learned how to perform a task then three years later when I try to do it again, have completely forgotten! Some folks may struggle with retaining information, especially obscure data we don't use daily. I've found that taking notes is absolutely critical to retaining knowledge. Another great benefit of smartphones, most include note taking features and if necessary, one can always snap a photo. Just the very act of writing things down will generally help recall the information later.

This is especially true when consulting a tax or financial advisor. If pen and paper is not out when an advisor is talking, you are wrong! Take good notes that are understandable when discussing with a partner at the dinner table later. Building knowledge is absolutely useless if it's quickly forgotten!

I want to reiterate knowledge of all sorts, has one thing in common, it equals money. Both directly such as in the case of a job promotion due to acquiring additional certifications as well as indirectly such as when we learn to do it yourself. Additionally, seeking knowledge is not something we pursue just in the four or five years immediately following high school. This truth is a lifelong endeavor. We will pull on these threads more as we cover our last tips to help realize financial truths to become a millionaire.

TIP #25: Gain and continually develop soft skills

Soft skills generally have limited or no official certifications as they are more personal attribute, yet they must still be learned. Oftentimes an employer, bank or business assumes that an individual possess a certain set of soft skills. Seldom are these skills included on a resume, but may be highlighted during interviews if there is a specific strength. Soft skills are an important piece of knowledge for the worker millionaire to possess! Let me explain.

Surprisingly, there are folks today who struggle with basic communication skills. Some folks may still hunt and peck when they type on a keyboard. I can't imagine in 2020 there are those who can't type at least 20 or 30 words per minute! Back in the day, I took a typing class and am convinced it was the most useful course offered in high school! Today, my wife and I conduct 99% of our business on line. If we couldn't type, we could not communicate as efficiently as we do in our financial endeavors.

Some people refuse to learn the basics of social media, email and other internet based communications critical in today's work place and society. Still others have not familiarized themselves with the use of basic office software for word processing, spreadsheets and presentations. One cool thing about using office software, there is always something new to learn. I've found the best way to learn about these tools is to find a friend or co-worker who possesses abundant skill and is willing (and patient enough) to show all the neat tricks these programs feature.

Another soft skill that is quickly atrophying in today's society is oral communication. Picking up the phone or looking someone in the eye and just talking is becoming a lost art. If your default setting is to communicate via typing or texting, make a conscious effort to start talking again. To be fair, not everyone is born with the gift of gab, but if there are barriers that may be preventing oral communication with individuals or groups of people, seek the help needed to overcome the challenge.

Communication (written and oral) is just one of several soft skills but it is an important one to continually develop. Communicating effectively by today's standards will improve other soft skills such as people and social skills. You don't have to be an expert, but possessing soft skills is required in today's workplace and in modern life. Don't put yourself at a disadvantage by not taking the time to gain this critical knowledge.

TIP #26: Earn a relevant degree or certification

The words in this tip were chosen carefully. First let's dissect the word "earn" as it is used above. It's always annoyed me when I hear "they received their electrician's license" or "she received her master's from state university". They didn't receive that education, they *earned* it!

This is an important distinction and permeates every aspect of gaining knowledge. Knowledge must be earned not simply received. For those of us who have attended a night class after a long day's work, attended a seminar on the weekend or had our nose buried in a book until well past midnight, you know what I am talking about. Like just about every concept we've covered in this book, gaining knowledge takes dedication and a commitment. From now on I challenge you to always use the word "earn" when talking about gaining knowledge!

Earning implies ownership of the knowledge and we value what we own. Too often when we are young, we miss this crucial point about knowledge. How many of us skated through high school just to be done with it? My mantra in college was "2.0 and go" since I knew I'd be serving in the military immediately after graduation. What a waste! Even though I earned a piece of paper, I really can't tell you the first bit of knowledge I gained during my college courses. Knowledge is earned, treat newly found knowledge with the respect it deserves.

Now let's look at the second carefully chosen word within this tip, *relevant*. There are two contexts to which "relevance" applies to a degree or certification. First, let's look at the most obvious context. Put simply, relevant education will enable the owner to find or perform a job better. Employers are looking for someone with at least a basic level of formal education and knowledge in a particular field. This certainly doesn't invalidate knowledge gained through experience, but relevant education will help get your foot in the door.

I didn't fully understand this important fact until I made the transition back to the civilian workforce after serving nearly a quarter century in the military. I majored in Aerospace Technology in college because I've always been fascinated by airplanes. Even though the program required a minor in mathematics which included taking calculus and differential equations, it was not an accredited engineering program, thus the "technology" moniker.

I quickly discovered in college I was in over my head as I am just not hardwired to excel at math. How many of us truly know ourselves that well at 19 years old? Being a little hard headed, I refused to change majors. Fortunately, I was able to slug it out and earn my Bachelors of Science degree, albeit with a very low GPA (recall my earlier comment about 2.0 and go).

Flash forward a quarter century as I am transitioning out of the military and trying to find a job. Mentally, I had kind of written off that not so impressive Aerospace degree from several years ago. But, as I started to look at education requirements for certain government and defense industry jobs, a recurring key criteria was "technical degree" usually defined as a number of courses in advanced math and engineering fundamentals. My little Aerospace degree met the technical education requirements for most of the jobs I was applying for! Coupled with my military experience, it made me a strong candidate. Thankfully, I was able to interview for several positions within the defense industry and pick the post military job that was right for me.

Of course, I couldn't solve a calculus problem right now if my life depended on it, but that's not the point. My degree met the basic education requirements for the jobs I applied for. If it hadn't, I wouldn't have even made it past the initial screening! My resume and application would just be tossed in the dreaded "not qualified" pile.

I learned quite accidently and much later in life that it does matter what is in that transcript so ensure education is relevant. I'll probably hurt some feelings here, but that "General Studies" Bachelor's degree may not meet some employers' basic education requirements. The same holds true for the professional trades. You obviously can't apply as an electrician, plumbing, truck driver or any other licensed position without the basic and sometimes advanced specialized credentialing. Earn *relevant* education and knowledge to open doors as well as increase earning potential throughout a working career. Above all, it's never too late to start seeking degrees and certifications!

Let's look at the other context for "relevant" degree or certification as it is used in this tip. In fact, I've already touched on it! Knowledge gained through formal education or certifications should be relevant not only to an employer, but more importantly *relevant for you*. This really comes down to an important life skill for all of us, being self-aware.

I mentioned earlier how my college age, hard headed self, chose a major I was not hardwired to excel in. It wasn't until a number of years later when I had the opportunity to complete a graduate degree in counseling did I learn that I am better suited for soft sciences. Hindsight is always 20/20, but I often wonder if I had been a little more introspective in my college age years and studied a subject *more relevant to me*, how my professional life would have turned out.

It is human nature and probably a little bit of American can do spirit that often keeps us charging ahead on a certain path because we think it's the right thing to do. It is important to stop and reflect from time to time in order to ask ourselves, am I (or will I ever be) really good at this? Will I be content performing this skill for a living?

I am so very thankful I landed in the military profession for my first career. I often wonder where my life would have headed if I had secured a job in the Aerospace industry with my mediocre degree and poor academic performance. I am quite confident I would have been miserable and probably ended up changing careers which can often be a time consuming and costly endeavor.

Strive to know yourself. If you aren't the helping others type, the medical field probably isn't a good fit, no matter how good the pay is. If you are like me and can't run a straight bead of caulk, being a successful house painter could be a challenge. Don't be afraid to admit you've chosen an area of learning or skill that may never work out. Have the courage to pursue the education and certifications that are *relevant* for you.

TIP #27: Make a commitment to lifelong learning

I know, I already mentioned this but it can't be stressed enough. There is a reason I am placing lifelong learning as the final tip. If there is anything to be gleaned from this book, it is remember to always seek knowledge. It is not only a truth to build wealth, it will help in so many other aspects of life. We are never too old to learn!

So what is lifelong learning besides a catchy tag line and why is it important? Well, like many things we've already covered, I will go to my military experience for a definition. Many would be surprised to learn the military places an incredible emphasis on the pursuit of knowledge and lifelong learning. I was a bit skeptical of the whole "warrior-scholar" concept when I first joined the military but after two decades I definitely became a true believer!

In my 24 year career, I spent *four years* in academic environments! This is in addition to my pre military education as well as numerous short term, technically focused training courses. These four years were spent in academic environments either on a college campus or very similar. We weren't learning how to blow things up better, for the most part, we were learning "how" to think.

Important to mention, I was drawing my military pay during these learning opportunities. The military was footing the bill entirely. I share this not to boast, but to illustrate how important learning and seeking knowledge is to our nation's military. The military whose job, at a very basic level, is to break things and fight, invests an incredible amount of time and treasure to ensure their leaders never stop learning.

So I guess you can say lifelong learning was kind of ingrained in me during my former profession! How does this translate into our everyday life? Well first, I've found to be a lifelong learner, you must be an active listener. I try to listen as best I can to others. I am fortunate to be able to retain and recall much of what I hear. As previously mentioned I also am an avid note taker. There are so many professionals out there who will gladly share their knowledge but it's only useful when we listen and retain. I've said it once and I'll say it again, if not taking notes when engaging with a professional, then you are wrong!

Active listening goes beyond professionals we may encounter in our investing or financial lives, it includes everyone. Take the time to listen to the talkative cashier at the grocery or department store. Slow down and spend some time with the elders in your life. This simple act of kindness will probably make their day and hopefully bring some good Karma into yours. More importantly, everyone has a unique perspective and it is often surprising what we can learn from the waiter or waitress who has something they need to get off their chest!

In addition to being an active listener to enable lifelong learning, we must be an active reader. When I was a kid my parents bought me a set of 1969 World Book encyclopedias. Mind you, this was 1983 so the info was already 14 years old! But in the pre-internet, pre-cable TV days, when there was nothing more exciting to do, I would often find myself reading these encyclopedias for hours. I know, pretty nerdy but I gained a wealth of knowledge. A few years later that extra knowledge helped me make my high school quiz bowl team (even nerdier, I know). Competing on my high school quiz bowl team along with my slightly above average grades in high school were probably two of the strongest entries on my Army ROTC scholarship application.

I am not saying reading encyclopedias as a kid paid for my college, but then again, maybe I am! The point is, don't fill down time with media blather, excessive gaming or unproductive vegetating. Read and educate yourself, if not on one of the many financial topics we've covered in this book, on anything that will improve quality of life.

Lastly, in addition to the traditional means for gaining knowledge we've discussed such as listening, reading and seeking formal education or training, travel internationally as much as possible. But wait, isn't "be frugal" a truth? How can I travel if I'm saving every penny?

If applying some of the life hacks we've discussed in this book, such as the credit card technique to build travel rewards, international travel can certainly be within grasp for the worker. Similarly, considering how much we spend on the theme park or beach vacations here in the United States, one may find that international costs only a little more. Skip the domestic vacation for a couple of years to save up enough for a two week visit to Africa, Asia or Europe.

But why travel internationally? I've been fortunate to earn a Bachelor's degree and two Masters, but some of the best educational experience I've encountered has been during my travels overseas. Traveling abroad broadens our perspective on so many things in our daily life. First and foremost, we probably won't be feeling as sorry for ourselves when living frugally, many in the world don't have a choice.

Additionally, while there are some commonalities, most countries outside the U.S. have very differing views on personal finance. By talking to residents of a particular country, one can learn firsthand what universal medical care and education really means and the associated costs.

I am very fortunate to be the not so better half of an international couple. My wife is from South Korea and for the most part, we see eye to eye on all financial matters. But she has some unique perspectives that have helped shape and guide me on our road to build wealth.

Certainly not suggesting to jump into an international marriage! But the lessons learned observing those in other countries and just talking to the citizens often provides a better education than anything one can read in a book. Make it a priority to travel abroad. It is one of the best ways to become a lifelong learner.

Knowledge is money sounds a bit flippant but I can't stress this financial truth's importance enough. Like diligence and frugality, seeking knowledge is a personal attribute we must strive for that compliments the more goal oriented truths such as investing and real estate.

I have witnessed first-hand in my own family the pitfalls of not seeking education and training at every opportunity. I am so very grateful my family pushed me to seek knowledge. I am also thankful for the excellent opportunities the military provided to increase my education over the years and travel abroad.

Most importantly, I hope I never lose my thirst for knowledge. Once this truth becomes a part of you, it's a chronic condition! Seeking information and gaining knowledge not only has positive impacts on net worth, it makes us a better person.

And with that, we've examined the five financial truths to become a millionaire on a worker's budget and the 27 tips that help realize the truths. Don't worry, we still have plenty left to cover in order to ensure there are no questions about the power of investing, being frugal, owning real estate, being diligent and seeking knowledge!

Let's take a look at the final financial review of our notional subject. No surprise, at age 44 and after just 24 years of living the truths, our subject is worth $1.3 million! Note that this is a $600,000 jump from our last review. If all these numbers have gotten lost in the 100 or so pages of accompanying text, not to worry. The next chapter will provide a narrative to accompany the math.

Truths in Action Financial Review #5 (Ages 40-44)

Highlights: 401k contributions exceeding max pretax allowance (remainder of contribution is after tax dollars). Purchase single family home for $300000 (Use $60000 from taxable investment account for 20% down and finance $240000 at 3.5% for 30 years. Purchase another vehicle at 41 ($50000 at 0% for 72 months).

	Yearly Income and Expenses Age 32-36					
	Age	40	41	42	43	44
Income	Annual Pre Tax Income	117716	119482	121274	123093	124939
	Gross Rental Income Duplex #1	24000	24000	24600	24600	25200
	Gross Rental Income Duplex #2	18000	24600	24600	25200	25200
Invest	401K (employee contr. exceeds max tax deductible)	27000	27000	27000	27000	27000
	Taxable Investment	15000	10000	10000	10000	10000
	Child #1 529 plan	2400	2400	2400	2400	3000
	Child #2 529 plan	1800	1800	1800	1800	2400
Expenses (Out)	Taxes / Withholding	23543	23896	24255	24618	24988
	Health & Dental Insurance	5000	5100	5100	5200	5200
	Mortgage #1 (Principle, Interest, tax, insurance)	16700	16700	17000	17000	17100
	Mortgage #2 (Principle, Interest, tax, insurance)	14700	14700	15000	15000	15200
	Mortgage #3 (Principle, Interest tax, insurance	9600	19200	19500	19500	20000
	Home repairs and upkeep	3600	3600	3600	3600	3600
	Car 1 & 2 (payment, ins, gas, & maintenance)	4000	12000	12000	12200	12200
	Cell Phone and Utilities	5000	5000	5100	5100	5200
	Food	12000	12000	12500	12500	13000
	Remaining for Everything Else*	19373 (1614/mo)	14686 (1224/mo)	15219 (1268/mo)	16975 (1415/mo)	16451 (1371/mo)

*Everything else includes clothing, entertainment, other needs and building small surplus in checking.

Investments Summary

Investment Accounts	
Compounded at 5% annually	Value at age 44
401K (+50% employer match)	665281
Child #1 529 Plan	39219
Child #2 529 Plan	24030
Taxable Investment	96942
Total Investment Accounts	825472

Property #1 Purchased age 29	
Value at purchase	190000
Down payment	10000
Principle remaining age 44	110440
Value age 44 (3% Appreciation)	296014 (+106014)
Real Estate Equity	185574

Property #2 Purchased age 33	
Value at purchase	190000
Down payment	38000
Principle remaining at age 44	112312
Value age 44 (Appreciation)	270894 (+80894)
Real Estate Equity	158582

Property #3 Purchased age 40	
Value at purchase	300000
Down payment	60000
Principle remaining at age 44	216169
Value age 44 (Appreciation)	347783 (+47783)
Real Estate Equity	131614

Final Net Worth Roll Up	
Investment Accounts	825472
Real Estate Equity	475770
Total Net Worth Age 44	**1301242**

Chapter 7: Truths in Action

In the introduction, I asserted math would prove out the effectiveness of the five financial truths. To accomplish this, I made certain assumptions about a notional subject and then provided "financial reviews" for our subject every five years. Hopefully you've been following the reviews at the end of each chapter and making your own conclusions about the truth's effectiveness!

It is a lot to digest, I know. In this chapter, I'd like to offer a narrative to accompany our financial reviews. A "word picture", if you will, to accompany the absolute certainty of the math. First, let's go back to the beginning and review the overarching assumptions we made about our notional subject.

Our subject begins their journey at 20 years old with a high school diploma and 15 hours of community college. They are single, living with roommates and employed full time as an hourly wage earner. They've got $1000 in savings and a brand new, compact SUV ($20000 financed at 4.5% for 60 months). Our hero is steadily banging out a bachelor's degree at a reasonably priced local college part time that they will complete at age 26. We've assumed they receive 100% financial aid, resulting in no student loan debt.

In the fourth year of the review, at age 23, our subject selects a partner and remains with them for the rest of their life. To keep things simple, our subject's partner will remain a homemaker. The happy couple will introduce two offspring at age 27 and 30. They don't keep any pets.

Another key assumption we made about our subject starting out is that they didn't make any big mistakes in the early years and have a fair to good credit score in the 600 range. Their continued pattern of financial responsibility will grow to an outstanding credit score in later years.

The actual place of employment for our subject is really irrelevant but we will assume they remain employed and continually increase in job responsibility as well as income. We factored in a fairly generous 1.5% pay raise per year to offset inflation. Finally, our subject remains with employers who offer all the typical basic benefits to include paid time off, health and dental insurance as well as 401k with employer matching.

You may recall a point in this book where we talked about location, location, location when it comes to real estate and cost of living. Our subject has chosen to settle their family in areas of the country where moderate costs for rent, insurance, utilities, gas, groceries, etc.... still exists. I'll reiterate, it will be challenging to build a million dollar net worth if living in an area where rent and cost of living exceeds national averages!

The next few assumptions about our subject are some things over which they don't have complete control, but must consider. First, we assumed our subject and their family remained in reasonably good health. No big medical concerns above what their insurance covered.

If death is one certainty in our lives, taxes are the other. Our subject takes full advantage of maxing out their 401k and investing in 529 plans for the offspring. Additionally, income gained from real estate investments is also tax advantaged. Our subject was taxed at 15% the first 10 years and 20% thereafter. Below is a breakdown of the tax rates we used in calculating our subject's financial reviews.

- 8% (10% after 10 years) withholding for FICA Social Security and Medicare
- 5% (8% after 10 years) *effective* federal income tax rate
- 2% *effective* state income tax rate

We figured property, sales and any other taxes within our annual expenses. I know, this isn't exact, but I daresay it is pretty close.

Lastly, we need to make some key assumptions about return on investments. I avoided the planning factor of a 10% annual return we see on some of the financial planning strategies and went with a more conservative average of 5% per year after all investment fees. Additionally, for our subjects' real estate investment portfolio, we assumed a fairly modest 3% increase in property value per year.

    I won't belabor the point I made at the beginning of the book. These assumptions won't fit everyone's circumstances, but they will fit many. If a particular set of real life circumstances doesn't fit perfectly with the assumptions for our notional subject, not to despair, the truths will still work! This will become more evident as we review the review. On that note, please feel free to flip back and forth to the financial review tables at the end of each chapter as we add the narrative to complete the story. So let's dig in...

    Our subject starts their journey towards millionaire status in their early 20s just trying to make a living. Thanks to fully espousing the five financial truths, they will make some great decisions along the way! They are grossing $35k a year or about $670 per week (a little over $15 an hour) with full benefits at the beginning of our review. Not too shabby for the average American just starting out. Especially when considering they are splitting rent with roommates!

    They are already socking away money into a short term taxable investment account as well as their employer's 401k for retirement. After all expenses, our subject still has about $150 a week left over to do the things single people enjoy doing. Life is good. We see them working hard and earning a small promotion to team leader at age 23 which puts them earning over $40k a year gross.

    Our subject feels this is probably the right time to ask their significant other to join them as a life partner. Congratulations! Thankfully, they dated for a number of years and financial truths featured prominently in their long talks. Our subject's partner is like minded and although it's time to ditch the roommates and low rent, our couple fight the urge to go out and buy the first house and new car they can afford. They choose instead to find another small apartment and keep the old reliable vehicle. As we mentioned, our subject's partner has chosen to stay busy at home, keeping up with all the household tasks and blogging in their spare time instead of seeking employment.

Even though at age 24 our hero is making over $43K per year, the size of the household has doubled! Everything costs almost twice as much now, health insurance, utilities, transportation and food. Regardless, our couple stay the course and buckle down to keep saving at the same rate, $100 per month in their taxable investment account and $150 per month into the employer 401k which as mentioned, offers matching contributions. This is frugality at its best, leaving only a small margin of $150 per week for life's "everything else".

In five years from age 20 to 24 our subject and their partner are off to a great start. We close this epoch with them possessing a net worth of almost $24k which includes $15k in their 401k retirement account and a little over $8k in their short term taxable "savings" investment account.

Our subject finally pays off their car at age 25 and the night college classes pay off. Our subject proudly walks across the stage after earning a Bachelor's degree in business management at age 26. Almost immediately, doors start opening and they get a hit on the resume they've been floating around. Our subject finds a new job as a junior manager in the similarly sized, next town over. Although they could afford a modest single family home, our subject keeps the "collect rent, don't pay it" truth in mind and holds off on buying a house. They've got bigger plans, and move into a two bedroom apartment *for the time being*.

Our couple is earning over $50k a year now and no car payment. Life is really good! But instead of blowing that extra income on wants, our frugal couple double down on investing. Over the next four years our subject increases 401K contributions to $300 per month and saves $200 per month in their taxable investment account. They are going to need it as some big changes are coming...

At age 27 our couple welcomes their first offspring to the family! Almost immediately, they open a college savings 529 plan and start saving $50 a month for the child's education. Things start happening rapidly as those of us who have started a family know. The two bedroom apartment is getting cramped and a second vehicle is needed for errands and appointments while our subject is at work.

Because our couple pays their bills on time and established good credit, they are able to find a great deal on a brand new compact SUV. They sell $5k from the taxable account for the down payment and are able to get a great 2.9% rate on a five year loan for the remaining $20k. That was easy!

After work each night, our subject has been diligently seeking knowledge on the rental and real estate market in their town focusing in on an area that has good schools and a mix of recently constructed single family and multi-family housing. Our couple made the decision to make their first home purchase an investment and chose not to look at the cute single family homes. When they see a duplex with three bedrooms and two baths on each side come on the market for $195,000 they are ready to jump!

At the age of 29, with good credit, and steady employment, our couple has a pre-qualification letter from the bank for a great 3.85% FHA backed home mortgage and has their $10k down payment ready to go from their taxable investment account. They make an offer and go under contract for $190,000. Congratulations, our hero is now both a homeowner AND a landlord.

For just a moment, our subject's partner looks longingly at the cute subdivision just across the street as they move belongings into their side of the duplex. Then their tenant's first $900 rent check comes in. This nearly pays the entire mortgage, insurance and property tax payment of $1200! That first year, they gross nearly $5400 in rental income and the value of their home goes up by 3%.

As if life couldn't get any better for this small family, after nearly five years at the new employer, they are promoted to management and earn a substantial raise. Our family is now earning over $75k a year in work and rental property income just shy of their 30th birthday!

But remember, these folks are ardent followers of the financial truths we've covered in this book. They are always seeking knowledge to make every dollar go as far as it can. With their expanding family, there is very little time to "veg out" in front of the TV. Their diligent minds are working overtime to make ends meet. Expenses have certainly risen to be sure, but they are keeping a close eye on it. They've managed to keep food / diapers down to $600 per month and utilities to just shy of $400. When something breaks in their new home or rental unit, our hero fixes it which keeps home maintenance costs down to $50 per month.

Living the truths stretches that $75k incredibly far. If they were undisciplined, they would be spending on frivolous wants, but our "power" couple understands they are firmly on the path to millionaire status. They know "investing early and often" is what it will take to realize the time value of money. At the end of this epoch, they are saving over $800 per month in their 401k and $500 per month in their taxable investment account. They are also getting a head start on their child's education by saving $50 per month. Before age 30 our subject has amassed a net worth of $90k, including over $70k in investments and over $18k in real estate equity.

This takes incredible discipline to be sure. The tight budget we've just covered leaves less than $200 per week for "everything else". That probably equates to arranging a sitter, and going on date night maybe once a month at the most. But these sacrifices in their twenties are about to start paying big dividends. Let's look at how the thirties treat our couple.

Our subject enters their 30s in a new decade, new tax bracket and a rapidly expanding family! At age 30 the family grows to four with the addition of another child. Just like with their firstborn, our subject opens a 529 college plan almost immediately. Their side of the duplex is starting to get a little tight but the kids are still small and it's working for now.

At age 33 they pay off their second car and old reliable, which is now 13 years old, is still running strong. Our subject knows the secret to extending the life of a vehicle is good preventative maintenance and of course, they do it all themselves. At 33 our hero also earns a pretty good raise at work. They are diligent workers in every sense of the word and extremely efficient. Management at the company is starting to take notice.

But work doesn't stop at 5pm when they leave the office. Every night after tucking the kids in bed our couple dedicates an hour to increasing knowledge through self-study. The topics vary, but most often its real estate focused. They love collecting rent and not paying it plus the rental market in their city is booming!

When a distressed, bank owned duplex hits the market they are ready to strike. Using $37k from their taxable account they are able to put 25% down and get a great 4% loan for the investment property. The property needs some work but after a couple of long weekends painting and fixing, the units are ready to rent.

At age 34, the couple is pulling in a little over $33k in gross rental income per year, but due to the great tax advantages for "passive" rental income, it does not impact their tax burden significantly. Our subject is now making over $84k at their employer so just shy of $120k per year total gross income yet they remain "super savers". By age 34 our subject is maxing out their 401k contributions at $20k per year which helps with tax burden. They still put about $800 a month in their taxable investment account as "savings" for the big purchases in life and they've been steadily increasing both kids' monthly 529 contributions which are up to $100 per month for child 1 and $50 per month for child 2.

The early 30s were a little lean. At one point, the "everything else" dipped down to under $200 per week for a family of four! But by age 34 the family has reached what they consider a comfortable standard of living. Even with steadily increasing expenses for food, utilities and transportation, the family has about $300 left over every week. They've deprived themselves for a while and now it's time to give into a few wants. The seven and four year old will love the big theme park vacation they've planned this year. The couple is finally able to buy some of the new clothes and furniture they've been needing.

You may recall, just before our subject's 30th birthday, their net worth was a respectable $90k. Now, at age 34 their net worth has increased to over triple that amount! Proof why investing early / often and owning real estate are such important truths to build wealth. Of the $325k in net worth, over $200k is in investment accounts and $120k in real estate equity. Just 14 years into our subject's journey to be a millionaire and they are almost a third of the way complete. Let's continue following the story.

At 35 our subject looks in the mirror and sees the tell-tale signs of hard work and stress. Those bags and tufts of gray hair didn't get there from just sitting around and relaxing. The couple decides to hold what they got for a couple of years and focus on the family. Raising two elementary age children, managing three rental units and working full time at a successful career is quite enough!

But life happens and at age 35 our subject's old reliable vehicle they bought at age 20 finally dies. No problem. They sold some mutual funds from their taxable account and thanks to excellent credit, were able to get a $30k car loan at 0% financing for five years.

As their growing children approach middle school they are eating a lot! By age 39 the family is spending $1000 per month in groceries. While they reached the comfortable level at age 34 the nearly $300 they have left over every week for "everything else" is quickly taken up by clothes for growing children and child activity fees.

They've sacrificed a lot to arrive here. Outlet malls and clearance racks are the norm. Sometimes they missed the big game because they used antenna TV service instead of cable. Their furniture is serviceable and neat but small enough to fit in the duplex. The kids are growing big and strong because they eat home cooked meals, but sometimes they ask why they can't eat out all the time like their friends do. Our subject makes over $100k per year but still drives a 10 year old car!

Worst of all, because they live in one side of a duplex, they aren't able to host friends very often and when they do, there are those awkward moments when someone let's slip out, "I couldn't live like this". It's hurtful of course, but our subject and their partner just remember that they will be millionaires soon with nearly limitless options while most of their friends will still be struggling well into their 60s.

Still, the family is happy. The highlight of the year is the annual vacation. They've been putting all their living expenses every month on a hotel rewards card and paying the balance diligently. Not only do they maintain excellent credit, they have enough hotel points to book a week at a luxury resort hotel every year! In between work and rental property management, they are able to make plenty of quality family time on the weekends. They play in the back yard, go to festivals in the park and the annual 4th of July celebration downtown. Sometimes they go camping, hiking or fishing on the long weekends, anything outdoors. It's different than going to the Cineplex every weekend to watch the latest hits or to the crowded amusement parks, but they wouldn't change anything. Their 12 and 9 year old are doing great in school and growing up right.

One day, just shy of our subject's 40th birthday, their senior executive calls them in and offers a senior management position! The executive commends our subject for not only their hard work but also all the additional training they've completed over the years. Our subject worked hard as well as sought self-improvement and company leadership noticed. This promotion to senior management results in a raise to over $120k gross salary per year!

Back home, the family celebrates and knows immediately what they must do. Buy a new home! Thankfully, they've got over $80k saved up in their taxable investment account, the down payment won't be a problem. The search begins!

Just short of 40 our subject is maxing out 401k contributions and still "saving" over $800 a month in taxable accounts. The kids 529s are growing and at age 12 and 9 are worth $19k and $10k respectively. At 39 they've got $377k saved for retirement, better than most people in America and over $80k in a taxable investment account for short term financial goals.

The real estate investments are doing great as well. Not only has rental income steadily increased up to a gross of $35k per year, they've built over $220k in equity. All told, just shy of our subject's 40th birthday, they are worth $709k! Notice how that net worth more than doubled in just five years? Compounding kicks into overdrive as account balances increase. All the more reason to invest EARLY!

Just before our subject's 40th birthday, the family closed on a beautiful single family home for $300k. Because they put $60k down and got a great 3.5% rate on the $240k mortgage, there is plenty left every month for upgrades or decorating. It's in the suburbs and a little bit of a commute to work but thankfully, their duplexes lie along the route so they can claim mileage for tax purposes. It needed a little work, but thanks to the skills our subject developed over the years, do it yourself tasks are not a problem plus working on the home will be a fun family project. Most importantly, it's zoned for the safe and highly rated county schools. The family is already talking about putting in a pool!

The compact SUV they bought 12 years ago is showing its age and the kids really don't fit in it anymore. At age 41 our family, perhaps for the first time, splurge and purchase a luxury brand SUV. Thanks to their exceptional credit, they are able to finance $50k at 0% for 72 months.

On our subject's 45th birthday, they sit on the deck overlooking a big back yard where a backhoe sits ready to dig the hole for the pool. They are enjoying a beverage and reflecting on where they've been over the past 25 years. With both duplexes fully rented and their position in senior management, they are grossing over $175k per year. They look at the statement from their investment company and the 401k retirement account is worth $665k. Their oldest child, who will start college next year, has $39k saved for education that will be tax free as long as used for qualified expenses. Their younger sibling already has $24k saved for college in a few years. They won't have to barely eek out an education in night school! More importantly, they should be able to graduate college with zero student loan debt.

Then there is the other half of our subject's wealth, real estate. Not only are the two duplexes producing $50k per year in tax advantaged rental income, the properties have grown substantially in value. Including their primary residence, our subject has amassed $475k in real estate equity.

Our subject is a millionaire worth $1.3M. Probably more importantly than the dollar figure, our subject has options for their future that many American's unfortunately don't have. At age 45 with both kids college bound within five years, they've got their finances well in hand. It shouldn't be much of a problem to put both children through school with minimal debt which will give them a leg up as they embark on their own adult lives and financial journey.

Best of all, they have options about how long they want to work. Key to remember, they won't be able to access their retirement accounts until almost 60 or in about 15 years. If our subject maintains the trend of maxing out 401k contributions, the 401k will be worth well over $1M by the time they reach 60. Furthermore, the rental properties should also increase in value. Conservatively, our subject should have $1.5M to $2.0M in assets at age 60 and probably much more. Additionally, our subject should be able to begin drawing Social Security benefits at age 62.

Depending on the quality of life they wish to maintain in their golden years, our subject has the option of retiring at age 60 if not sooner. How awesome is that? Many Americans work until age 67. Not our example of the truths in action! Life is too short.

Our subject's path to millionaire status was a tough road but anything worth having usually is. Important to highlight that it would be absolutely impossible to achieve this milestone if our subject's partner wasn't completely on board. Sacrifice, especially in a family, is never a solo endeavor.

We've just examined the story of a notional American worker who started quite average, but ended up in the top 10% of American households by applying some simple truths in their financial lives. There were no magic formulas such as the "$50 per day for twenty years" method that we read about often. If you look at the numbers, there is no way our subject could have saved $50 a day back when times were lean.

The narrative we just reviewed runs counter to many people's financial journeys today. Most people don't like hearing it's going to take the average worker a lot of sacrifice and close to 25 years to amass a million dollars. Additionally, some may not view a million dollars in non-liquid assets such as retirement accounts and real estate as wealth. They would prefer to be sitting on a mountain of cash to do with as they see fit. But unless coming into a large sum of money, such as winning the lottery, the truth is most of us will never possess a million dollars in liquid assets. For the majority of us, our wealth will look just like our subjects, retirement accounts and real estate.

The themes and outcomes I have covered are grounded in reality. The truths in action review of our "notional subject's" journey to a million dollars mirrored much of my own journey and I am confident there are countless others who walked this same path to financial success.

Chapter 8: Final Thoughts

Many assert that what separates human from beast is free will. Humans possess the free will to obey or break laws, practice religion, hold ideals and love as they choose. The decisions we make about our financial lives are no exception. This is not to infer each of us are born with the same opportunities and that building wealth is simply a matter of choice. I don't believe that for one second. I do believe however, in America, the least of us still possess the capacity to create opportunity regardless of circumstances.

This is the only way I can explain my own family and the successes we have enjoyed. My grandparents were raised in borderline abject poverty in the South during the depression. They survived and were able to raise my parents to a better standard of living, but not quite middle class. When they died, they had enough in their estate to take care of final expenses and left no debt. I suppose for their generation and circumstances, they were financially successful.

My parents, applying the rudimentary financial truths taught to them, further raised the bar for me by providing a solidly middle, working class home. Yet they still didn't fully grasp some of the truths I've discussed in this book. For instance, although they understood the inherent value of education they didn't really know how to go about earning their own or saving for mine.

Fortunately, I was able to figure it out. My parents worked hard their whole lives and I don't have to worry about them as they are financially secure enough to remain comfortable well into their golden years. There may be some left of their estate when they are gone but that doesn't really matter. They were successful given the opportunities they created.

So that brings us to my generation! We are all products of our experience and I am no exception. You've probably picked up that my family's relatively meager beginnings and military service shaped me tremendously both personally and with regards to finance. I am very thankful for these defining experiences. I am even more thankful for being self-reflective enough to understand how these experiences enabled financial success. The five truths instilled by my family were certainly the foundation but my wife was the glue that brought it all together.

It was truly fortuitous for this small town American boy to meet such a like-minded Korean girl! While I will never be able to fully relate to what it was like for her growing up in hard times within a developing nation in the 1970s and 1980s, I know part of the success of our relationship is our shared view on the financial truths.

I can't stress enough that building wealth is a team sport. Partners always get a vote on financial decisions and it certainly helps when they vote your way! I think too often young people in love gloss over this important aspect of relationships. Many a marriage was doomed because of incompatible views on money. I am so blessed to have a wonderful partner!

Just entering our 50s, we have nine rental properties and are building one more. I still work and am blessed to have a great job. In my later 50s, once the kids get through college, I will evaluate whether to keep working or retire early. Our retirement savings will ensure we stay comfortable as long as we live and most likely there will be some left over as a legacy for the kids when we are gone.

Which brings me to the next generation in our family, my two boys. As our oldest prepares to enter college in 2022, I am so very proud that all he has to focus on is getting accepted to the institution of his choosing. He is a long way from where I was, wondering "how am I going to pay for this!" We opened 529 accounts for him and his brother when they were born and have been steadily increasing contributions over the years. For their part, they are excelling academically and at life in general.

My wife and I have tried to teach our two sons the financial truths that were ingrained in us. I think our kids get it, but I am very curious how the truths will manifest in their adult lives. "Being frugal", for instance, will look a lot different for them, than it did for us.

They've lived the truths in their childhood. Just like I wore my cousin's hand me downs when I was a kid, our youngest gets his brother's hand me downs. And one small detail I left out of the chapter on the truth "collect rent, don't pay it", I've got two great apprentices that work hard to help me paint, mow and repair our rental properties! We will see how the financial truths manifest in their lives. They are starting at a completely different level than my wife and I.

Perhaps that is the true meaning of "generational changing" wealth. Often I think we take this expression to mean passing on a huge inheritance when we die but I am not so sure anymore. With the advances in health care, most people live to be really old! Not to sound cold, but will our kids really care if we live to be in our 90s and pass them a large inheritance when they are in their 60s?

I think generational changing wealth is less about the sum of an inheritance and more about passing on to the next generation a progressive view on wealth they can use in their adult lives. Our children have many more opportunities than we did, but they also have instilled within them the financial truths passed on by generation. The way they live the truths will look differently for sure. I can't imagine our kids living in one side of a duplex! I can imagine them making their first home purchase from a financial perspective rather than an emotional one. I can see them buckling down in school because they understand that "knowledge is money." I certainly hope so!

The critic would contend my basis for the financial truths, mostly personal experience and little scientific research, is too narrow for a true validation. Additionally, they'd shoot holes in our "truths in action" review of a notional subject, mostly because my assumptions may omit some common life circumstances. I am ok with that.

I stated clearly upfront the assumptions made are for illustrative purposes. Divorces, illness, massive debt and accidents happen. Although I left life events such as these out of the assumptions, I also was very conservative on other assumptions. We based the whole study on a single earner. How many single earner households are left in America? We used a relatively modest rate of return for mutual fund and real estate investments.

Regardless, does it really matter if reaching a million dollar net worth at age 45, 55 or even 65? Millionaire status remains elusive for so many Americans today and it shouldn't. I hope the financial truths in this book will inspire someone covered up in debt or recently divorced. Don't give up on building a secure financial future and just start living paycheck to paycheck. As long as there is a source of income, anyone can start applying the truths!

The five financial truths and the tips that enable them are common sense and I probably didn't share anything new. Sometimes we all need a reminder of what's right in front of us. In case you've forgotten, let's go over them one last time. Additionally, at the end of this chapter there is a list of the truths and the twenty seven tips we reviewed for reference. This book is meant to be marked up, dog eared, and written in (or the e book equivalent of said actions).

Truth #1: Invest Early, Invest Often
To build wealth, saving must be a priority over a lifetime. This inevitably means giving up access to hard earned income during the here and now for use later in life. The time value of compounding money can never be underestimated. To be a millionaire on a worker's budget you must save aggressively your entire working life.

Truth #2: Be Frugal
To become a millionaire on a worker's budget, one must spend conservatively. This all comes down to understanding needs versus wants and showing self-control in *every purchase and financial move*. This is probably the hardest truth as it takes an incredible amount of patience, discipline and sacrifice.

Truth #3: Collect Rent, Don't Pay It
It will be a challenge for a worker to build a million dollar net worth in their forties if paying rent for 20 years. Moreover, real estate should be an important part of every investment portfolio. The benefits of real estate investing is no secret. But make no mistake, owning real estate is more than just an investment, it is a bona fide part time job!

Truth #4: Be Diligent
This is more than just working double shifts, we are all hard workers. To become a millionaire as a worker, diligence must become a life value. This means when something is broke, fix it…now. Never walk past a wrong, take immediate action. Get to yes or move on. These behaviors will make incredible impacts in all aspects of your life, especially in ability to earn.

Truth #5: Knowledge is Money
There are really two kinds of knowledge when related to finance. First, the knowledge gained through a commitment to lifelong self-study in order to make informed decisions. From the most basic daily purchases to which investment products are best, every single financial decision requires gaining knowledge and developing understanding. Second, is knowledge in the more traditional sense, formal education and training. Without a degree or a certified skill, a worker will have a hard time increasing earning potential over the years.

As I complete this book, our planet has been gripped by a global pandemic for a little over a year now. I think it's taken a toll on all of us in many different ways. Vaccines are beginning to roll out and for the moment, cases of infection are trending downward, but I am not sure anyone really knows if we turned the corner. Who knows if we will ever return to "normal" and what the long term impacts to our society will be. My assumption is "normal" will look much different in the future.

Our economy is in an unusual spot. Despite the pandemic, the stock market continues to trend upward and consumer spending remains steady. For large manufactured goods such as cars and appliances, demand is far exceeding supply due to COVID-19 impacts on production. People are still spending money.

As far as real estate goes, most markets are experiencing an incredible boom. In our particular area, homes stay on the market literally for a few hours before an offer is accepted. In our rental business, we can't rent vacant apartments fast enough. When we list a home for rent, we receive an overwhelming response from literally hundreds of qualified prospective tenants.

My dad, who is by no means a trained economist, used to say that the next depression would be just the opposite of the last. Everyone will have money, but be unable to purchase anything. Never was sure what he based this assertion on, but I am beginning to think perhaps he was on to something.

Lastly, there is social and political unrest not only around the world but right here in the United States. Change is a constant and most of the time needed. Some of the economic and political changes suggested these days would have fundamental impacts to our financial lives. I think what probably has most of us uptight about the recent turmoil is not necessarily the change itself, but the rhetoric surrounding it and fear of the unknown. Change is never easy.

I know it sounds elementary (then again, a lot in this book probably does), but when I feel myself getting anxious about current events, I reflect back on history. How was America able to unite and rebuild post-Civil War? How did society recover after the Spanish Flu pandemic of 1918? How did my grandparents overcome the hardships they faced as children during the depression? How did most every society on the planet recover from the devastation of WWII?

History shows that our societies not only survive these crucibles, but often thrive in the aftermath. Many of our best economic periods immediately followed man-made and natural disasters such as the roaring twenties or the 1950s post World War booms. We will get through today's uncertain times and be stronger for it!

And that is the great thing about truths. Truths are constants or as the dictionary puts it "facts accepted as true". Truths don't care about political ideologies or viruses. Regardless of how our economy or society will look on the back side of our current state of affairs, few can dispute that investing, real estate, frugality, diligence and knowledge are the necessary truths for the worker to build wealth.

I am not the most eloquent with words and witticisms, but the one pithy expression I like to remind my two boys of frequently is "everything, *absolutely everything*, in this life is the result of a decision". But wait, they ask, if someone dies in a plane crash, that wasn't their decision? They certainly didn't decide the time of their death but they did decide to get on the plane. Others may say, I didn't pick my parents, how was that a decision? True, but it was a decision to have you, just not yours. Everything that happens in life is the result of a decision.

Building wealth is about making good decisions. Unfortunately for us workers, we have to be quick and wise in our decision making to make our limited resources go further. The truths we've covered in this book can get you there. Fortunately, we've been blessed with free will to make decisions and create opportunities for ourselves. Make the decision to apply the five financial truths and get on track to a million dollar net worth!

Five Financial Truths and the tips to help espouse them

Truth #1: Invest Early and Often

- Close the savings account and open a taxable investment account with automatic investing for short term needs (3 – 5 years)
- Open and set up automatic investing in an employer's 401k (or a Traditional IRA); start 529 accounts for children as soon as they arrive
- Establish a comfortable standard of living, then put the amount of all future pay raises into an automatic investment plan
- Invest in others (a.k.a. give back)
- Use caution with life insurance and annuity "investments"
- Use windfalls to pay off bad debt or invest

Truth #2: Be Frugal

- Perform a "needs vs. wants" assessment before every purchase
- Right size your life, (a.k.a. avoid champagne taste on a beer budget)
- Learn how to do it yourself
- Bargain hunt, haggle and use coupons / discounts
- Eat at home a majority of the time and always carry lunch
- Put all monthly expenses on a rewards credit card, then pay the bill in its entirety when due
- Never, ever carry a balance on a credit card
- Control vices
- Beware the free lunch

Truth #3: Collect Rent, Don't Pay It

- The first rule of real estate is location, location, location; the second rule of real estate is location, location, location
- Understand financing options and don't be afraid to get creative
- Maintenance, repairs and the general cost of ownership must be kept under control to remain profitable in real estate investing
- Understand and leverage rental property income tax implications
- Investing in real estate is a people business; know tenants well
- Cover your assets

Truth #4: Be Diligent

- Never walk past a problem
- Find a way to get to yes or go in a different direction
- Always be on time and stop procrastinating

Truth #5: Knowledge is Money

- Gain and continually develop soft skills
- Earn a relevant degree or certification
- Make a commitment to lifelong learning

www.ingramcontent.com/pod-product-compliance
Lightning Source LLC
Chambersburg PA
CBHW061439040426
42450CB00007B/1120